The Gatekeeper's Key

Crossing Thresholds through Portals of Potential

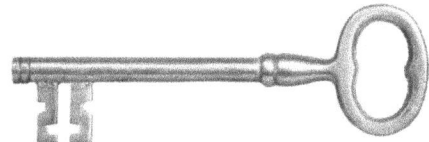

Kathryn Ross

Pageant Wagon Publishing
Vineland, NJ

Family Literacy Books

The Gatekeeper's Key:
Crossing Thresholds through Portals of Potential
By Kathryn Ross © 2017
Pageant Wagon Publishing
A Division of Pageant Wagon Productions, LLC
Vineland, NJ 08361

BISAC: *Religion/Christian Life/ Personal Growth*

ISBN: 978-0-9981771-1-3
www.pageantwagonpublishing.com

All Rights Reserved. Except for brief quotations in printed, blog, or social media reviews, no part of this publication may be reproduced in any other form. This includes electronic, mechanical, photocopying or recording for commercial use. This publication is for the personal use of the recipient only. Any extensive use of this material requires written permission from the author and publisher, except as provided by USA copyright laws.

Gatekeeper Endorsements

In these literature-rich story-world meditations, Kathryn Ross explores what it takes to step out of our comfort zones and go after the desires of our hearts. Using her own life and learnings as examples, she notes how various gates blocked her path to success. But using her Gatekeeper Keys, she conquered her fears and marched on to success. Use her keys to unlock the gates that block you from reaching your potential.

Janice Hall Heck, Co-Author/Editor, *Triumph Over Terror*
with 911Ground Zero Chaplain Bob Ossler

Kathryn is unique in her ability to persevere. In this book, *The Gatekeeper's Key*, you will discover what's behind the passion that keeps her going. If you love word studies and metaphorical stories, this short study will be an encouragement to you as you discover how to persevere even when things look hopeless. At the end of each section is a guided journal and discussion opportunity.

Lei Felmey, Administrative Assistant
Cumberland County Community Church, Millville, NJ

In literary style, Kathryn Ross has created a book that shows the value of forging ahead despite the obstacles of life that come. If you have felt like it's no use, you will appreciate that the author has been there, too, and you will discover the reason to go on.

Sal Roggio, Pastor
Cumberland County Community Church, Millville, NJ

I enjoyed *The Gatekeeper's Key* very much. It is written in a very creative way and I feel it keeps the reader interested. I recommend this book as it is inspiring and challenges the reader to rise-up and have courage to face difficulties, always trusting God for the results.

Chris Evans, Author/Historian
Odyssey of Faith: The Virginia Colony, Jamestown and You

Dedication

The barriers are not erected
which can say to [aspiring] talents and industry,
"Thus far and no farther."

Ludwig van Beethoven

To the many mentors in my life—from my most tender years to today: in success and failure, friends and 'frienemies', saints and sinners, in season and out. Polished professionals paved the way with footsteps before me. Gatekeepers all.

You invited me to seize my calling to "write His answer" and turn the key, unlocking God's purposes in my life and calling. Your deposits in my life pruned my character, expanded my vision, stretched my skills, and boldly challenged me to cross thresholds of platform, purpose, and potential in the ministry of words—written and spoken—for the glory of God.

Table of Contents

Introduction: The Dream ~ Page 3

Chapter 1 ~ Page 9
The Gatekeeper's Key

Chapter 2 ~ Page 27
The Key of Love: In Waiting, Know Patience

Chapter 3 ~ Page 39
The Key of Courage: In Acceptance, Embrace Confidence

Chapter 4 ~ Page 51
The Key of Faith: In Trust, Commit Obedience

Chapter 5 ~ Page 65
Gates and Glory: In Strength, Cross Thresholds

Chapter 6 ~ Page 79
Portals to Potential: In Opportunity, Go Forth

Chapter 7 ~ Page 91
One Way Through: Jesus—The Ultimate Gatekeeper

Appendix ~ Page 101
Defining the Terms Word Study

Notes ~ Page 111

About the Author ~ Page 113

~ The Gatekeeper's Key: Introduction ~

A single dream is more powerful
than a thousand realities.
J. R. R. Tolkien

Introduction
I Dreamed a Dream

I dreamed in sepia tones.
A watercolor wash of city skyscrapers.
Blurred.

In the foreground, a host of faceless people in dark silhouette squashed around me. We stood, barricaded by a wire fence. Thronging on the threshold. Massing on the margins. A bleak world as backdrop, we stared longingly through the wire web at the open fields wide with promise on the other side.

A voice behind me said, "Take the risk."

I couldn't tell where the voice came from, but it played the role of a light switch clicking my soul and spirit "on." As though waking, energized and alert, I sensed a change in the atmosphere. Clouds gathered above, heavy with expectation. The faceless shadows surrounding me did not notice or move in response.

But, I could no longer remain still. I looked closely at the wire barrier blocking me from stepping forward. It was a bold thing to inspect the insurmountable impediment, rather than simply accept it being there.

A closer examination revealed a transformative truth about the fence: chicken wire. Fine, frail, bendable chicken wire, stapled to light, thin slats of wood, sunk into the ground barely six inches.

This is nothing, I thought. *Why have I allowed this fragile fence to confine me all this time?*

I grasped the slat closest to me and pulled it back with ease, opening the way of escape like a gate. A Gate!

Like Dorothy in Oz, learning she'd always had the power to go home with the click of her heels, I'd positioned myself directly in front of the way out of my colorless waiting place the whole time—but I didn't see it until that providential moment. Like Dorothy, I had much to learn about brainpower, a cultivated heart, and true courage, before I'd be ready to go forth to my heart's desire.

Instantly the gathering clouds exploded in enormous billows, arresting my attention. "Look!" I shouted, pointing out the sight to others.

Light pierced the thick white, puffy swells, creating an open portal of sorts. Small flickering lights scurried through the cloud opening, hovering above the ground before us. Cherub faces materialized in the lights, flickering and bouncing about, their mouths moving in excitement as though rejoicing. I could not hear what they said. They leapt like my heart when punctured by the glory of sudden inspiration. The portal light widened, drawing me to it. Instinctively I sensed the presence of Jesus and called out to

~ *The Gatekeeper's Key: Introduction* ~

Him, lifting my arms, like a child beckoning her Daddy, to sweep me up in a strong embrace.

Daring to cross the boundary line, I advanced from sepia to Technicolor landscapes in the same way Dorothy stepped into Oz from the rural black and white of her Kansas kitchen. I raced towards a new world alive with color.

I woke and recorded the dream in my journal, wondering what it meant. That was in mid-August 2013, the same week I'd obeyed a prompt from the Lord to self-publish a book. Having entertained my love affair with literature and letters from my youth, I'd always dreamed I'd publish one day. My work for so many years had been confined to electronic files and three-ring binders. I lacked the knowledge to progress beyond small, local audiences in classrooms and close circles of loyal friends.

I lacked an Invitation from a Gatekeeper with a Key to turn the lock of a dream into reality.

But, in August 2013, the Invitation arrived. A Gatekeeper looked me square in the eye and proclaimed, "Take a risk. Step beyond your comfort zone. Upgrade your skill set. Face your fears. Pass through the gate. And here's the Key: Learn how to self-publish using CreateSpace."

You could have asked me to don a flight suit and launch a jet off the deck of an aircraft carrier for all I knew of such a thing. The temptation to shrink back swelled within me.

In the medieval schools of arts and trades, when the apprentice developed sufficient skill, the master sent him out as a journeyman to prove himself on his own, outside the walls and beyond the gates of mentoring. How would I fare on my own?

I did not know. My dream ended—open-ended—abruptly, without resolution as to what would happen next. Only the promise of His Presence going with me as I ventured beyond the previously fixed boundaries to an expansion of borders.

For so long the fences in my life were like barbed wire barricades, pinching me in pain when I tried to penetrate them. Trials discipline soul and spirit—temper and talent. But now, in my dream, the adversary fence turned out to be no more than flimsy chicken wire, easily breached.

Within four weeks, after much kicking, crying, digital meltdowns, mountains of error messages, failure notices, document rejections, and bouts of depression questioning the wisdom of risk-taking, I published a modest forty-page collection of old poems and a short story. I held a glossy 6x9 book with a spine in my hands with MY name on the cover. The impenetrable was penetrated. The Key to Publishing unlocked the gate, opening the way forward to another fence. A wall, in fact. And another gate therein to which I should make my way as a journeyman proving my worth, in search of more mentors, masters, and Gatekeeper Keys to the purpose. Going forth, I knew more risk loomed ahead.

The landscape on this new journey was not as sepia-toned as before. But each stumbling step along the way drained some color from the vista around me as I struggled. I covered rocky terrain, wetlands, parched deserts, dark forests, hills, valleys, and foreboding dangers in big cities on this path. Success and Failure traveled by my side as I met new walls and gates of varied styles.

I was never alone. Always in His Presence, with an Invitation, a Gatekeeper, and a Key—perhaps more than one. I learned to submit to each along the way.

That's My Story—What's Yours?

Whether you dream about publishing books, opening a business of your own, seeing yourself on the other side of a mountain of health issues, resolving strained family relationships, or seeking a life goal that seems out of reach, you need to find the mentors and gatekeepers in your life with the key to help you make dreams come true.

I explore these themes in this book through metaphorical short story and inspirational essays using personal testimonies, excerpts from classic literature, visual imagery, challenge questions for discussion, and journal prompts. You are encouraged to first review the Word Study in the Appendix as preparation to chapter reading and follow-up.

If you've ever felt stuck in a gated confine, unable to cross the threshold through the portal of your potential into the field of your hopes and dreams—your goals and life calling—then use these story-world meditations as a ray of light to help you discern your place and season. May you recognize His Voice when He invites you to take risks and boldly pass through gates to grow into greater things.

Kathryn Ross
February 2017

~The Gatekeeper's Key: Chapter 1—The Gatekeeper's Key ~

She knew opportunity lay beyond the gate, but so did a whole new level of risk in evaluations and rejections.

The Gatekeeper's Key

Chapter 1: The Gatekeeper's Key

The four head gatekeepers, all Levites, were in an office of great trust, for they were responsible for the rooms and treasuries in the Tabernacle of God.
TLB

They were responsible for the security of all supplies and valuables in the house of God. They kept watch all through the night and had the key to open the doors each morning.
The Message
1 Chronicles 9:26-27

nce upon a time there was a wall with a gate separating a vast Field of Dreams from the inhabitants living in Wannabe Village.

Therein, an artist resides.

She weaves words. A love of texture swirls about in her soul. She captures them, taming their fibers in her imagination until they are useful in spilling from her lips with sound, or her fingers to the printed page.

The wonder of letter threads, deftly handled and woven together into connecting cords, form her words. In this way, the intangible nature of meaning and thought find a highway to understanding and apt communication. A powerful craft through which to transform lives.

Clutching her words, kneading them, ripping them from one place to another, Weaver works them like a bird feathering a nest in anticipation of a new creation. Something of herself is born through the work of her words. She must master excellence in her craft 'ere her words prove a poor representation of the great things she thinks.

When Weaver mounts her threads and cords on the loom, she shuttles them about, lining them up just right, each atop the last. One between, over and under another. In this way, her words weave sentences.

She strings sentences together with more threads. Stronger threads and three-fold cords become yarns—spools of thought spun in the energy of Weaver's inventiveness.

Paragraph skeins link like chains, following the pattern of a concept working in Weaver's mind, soul, and spirit. Thoughts organized into the theme of a tale hold all things together. Word pictures develop, providing the framework of activity for characters, plots, and motives of the heart.

Some days, Weaver sings as she shuttles her words, sentences, and paragraphs to their assigned place. An idea, well fashioned, pours like water from a pitcher into a glass, splashing gleefully onto a page of record.

But there are days when her texts ebb and flow as the tide. A wave wild with bubbling foam washes up, leaving a deposit of colorful word threads and loops of yarn paragraphs. Then, just as swiftly as they formed, they stall and recede. Weaver knows they will come again to the shore of her understanding, but the wait is prone to frustrate.

~The Gatekeeper's Key: Chapter 1—The Gatekeeper's Key~

In such industry, Weaver plies her trade as a resident in Wannabe Village, enclosed roundabout by Muchado Wall, so named for the many fear-filled blocks cemented one onto another, as though a tumult of complaint. Built thick and high through the years with unnumbered bricks hardened in the ovens of Treadmill Kilns, this formidable fencing confines as much as comforts.

For some in Wannabe, the daily work routine allotted to them in their craft is enough sustenance to be going on with. They keep to their comfort zones at the center, giving little thought to worlds outside, knowing only of what they see in the scope of their narrowed vision. With hands to work and eyes cast down, some live their entire lives unaware of any wonders beyond their village. Blissfully ignorant, they toil. Safe and secret. Unburdened by a want of more in the shadow of Muchado.

Except for the residents on the outskirts.

These fence-sitters are the restless ones who have glimpsed beyond Muchado Wall through cracks in its mortar. The Field of Dreams lies on the other side. Once sighted, seeds implant within hearts. A sense of calling roots within souls. These citizens of Wannabe are never the same again. Desire to breach the wall's limitations spurs their work in such cases. They set off to relocate outside the village center, to the border streets nearest the only place of coming in and going out: The Gateway of Greater Things.

Here, on the fringe of Wannabe Village, is where Weaver lives on Waiting Lane. She has resided there for some time, bemoaning her lack of skill, entertaining old Mistress

Doubts-A-Lot at teatime, more often than not. When she returns to her efforts in the aftermath of their repast, she notices her clumsy fingers drop words. She misses stitches, making her story uneven. Letters, jots, and tittles fall out of place. Perhaps she has overindulged on the scones.

In truth, an upgrade in tools and training is wanting, but she lacks the means to acquire them, the resolve to the purpose, and the wisdom in how best to employ them on her story loom.

To that end, she labors in the paradox of both joy and unrest in her calling. Her tapestries of tales show promise. Yet, her lack of a Master Story-Weaver to mentor her efforts towards greater purpose stirs bouts of despair in her heart.

She knows where to find him. The Master. He is the Gatekeeper to the Field of Dreams so near her home. The Gatekeeper holds the Key of Opportunity. It is a key she has long desired, but shrinks back from fully pursuing.

One day, Weaver ventures into the marketplace where words and tapestries trade hands. There, in the midst of so many tales, stands the Gatekeeper. The Master Story-Weaver himself! Other eager weavers reach out to him in a flood of tales. Some limp about, tripping over their words for all the loose threads and yarns, falling flat on the ground before him. Others push and shove, staking a claim by his side, petitioning for a key that they might know the opportunities on the other side of the gate.

But, the treasuries therein are not to be toyed with, and the gate's portal not to be opened to aggressors. The

Gatekeeper knows the worth of each word tapestry laid before him and allows only those who prove themselves worthy of the key to have access. By invitation.

Even so, it is clear to everyone what tribute must be brought in proving oneself. They read these words etched on the gate's signpost:

PURPOSE
Prove purpose to me—that you know your calling;
For only the called gain the key.

PRODUCT
Display your passion in what you produce;
A product I will have to see.

PERSEVERE
Show fearless effort! Face your foes to the finish;
Persevere in the fray, do not flee.

Weaver has spent a lifetime tending her threads and yarns and looms. Her reputation in the village is inextricably linked to such pursuits. Many have been gifted with her word tapestries in one form or another, for she delights to sow her words beyond herself. On occasion, she blesses those in need of warmth, hope, and healing, wrapping them in the tightly woven fibers of her tales. There is always a risk of rejection, to be sure, for bearing one's heart and art through the works of one's hands opens the door to evaluation. But, as her skills develop, her confidence in such ministry grows—though slowly. She remains selective in publishing her works abroad to a wider audience.

Recipients of her weaving regularly encourage her to seek out the Gatekeeper for the Field of Dreams on the other side of Muchado Wall, crossing the threshold through the Gateway to Greater Things.

"You *should* petition the Gatekeeper for an invitation," says one.

"If only you *would* ask, you just may receive," admonishes another.

"You *could* be so much more if you just stopped inviting that old Mistress Doubts-A-Lot to tea," declares yet another well-meaning advocate.

Weaver wears their praise with a smile, half wishing to leave, yet dreading the thought of leaving her cozy apartment on Waiting Lane. She knows opportunity is only possessed beyond the gate, but, there too, she knows she'll confront a whole new level of risk in evaluations and rejections. Lingering on the fringe must suffice for the moment. No amount of wouldas, shouldas, and couldas seem potent enough to convince her otherwise. She has no surety that the benefits of expanding her tapestry's borders would be equal to the risk. Still, the fact remains: No one becomes a Master Story-Weaver apart from crossing the threshold of the portal to potential—the Gateway of Greater Things.

Weaver sighs. She so desires to be a Gatekeeper holding keys herself, some day.

Silently, she stands, observing the frenzied activity of the throng of weavers boldly attempting to storm the gate. Some hold invitations from the Gatekeeper. But those without invitations either fumble or rant about, in competitive attempts to force themselves into position before they have honed their skills to prove worthy. This provides sufficient reason for her to tuck away her own ambitions and cower on the sidelines. Watching. Fearing she might be poorly skilled and unworthy, herself.

Weaver has yet to receive an invitation.

Cheers rise-up now and again when the Gatekeeper grants a worthy recipient a Key of Opportunity. Oh, the wonders they will own for their tapestries and future word weavings! They have been brave enough to take hold of the invitation, to seize opportunity for themselves, and to go forth into their Field of Dreams through the Gateway of Greater Things. Perhaps their work will be displayed within castle halls and exhibited far and wide in the company of other approving Master Story-Weavers.

She is happy for them. But her heart aches all the more for remaining on this side of the gate, no key in her hand. And no invitation forthcoming. The works of other weavers distract her. She admires their tales and gleans valuable treasure threads from them to add to her crafting tools. But others stir a froth of despair in her heart when she measures her worth by their weavings.

Today, like every day, the Gatekeeper holds court by his portal. She watches from a safe distance in the shadows at the end of Waiting Lane, holding her best tapestry close to her. Across the yard, she sees the Key of Opportunity shimmering in the sunlight, hanging from the Gatekeeper's belt. It beckons her to reach out and try for the prize.

The Gatekeeper slips his hand into a leather pouch hanging from his belt and pulls out a smattering of small envelopes. The invitations! He passes them out to a few who petition him. She eyes the envelopes with desire—and trepidation.

Why does she waver and doubt her Purpose? Her Product is plentiful, the fruit of her loom, woven through years of Perseverance. Still she knows it lacks the polish of what opportunity alone could produce in it, nurturing it to full promise. As much as she desires to hold an invitation in her hand, she doubts she would accept it for all her fears.

If only she had not peeked through the crack in Muchado Wall that day long ago. She had wandered away from the village center and chanced to look up—and out—for the first time. A seed of hope and vision planted then, deep in her being. The present burden of cultivating its growth and improvement fatigues her. Shrinking back, she fears the Gatekeeper's evaluation might sting. She might fail. So, she lingers on the outskirts of Waiting Lane.

"Ugh! Is that all there is?" a word weaver grunts from behind her.

"Pardon me?" she says, turning to the voice, thinking she has committed an offense.

"This! THIS!" he brusquely waves a torn envelope and card over his head. "There's nothing to this! Nothing at all! A word. One word. No use to me."

Weaver follows the staccato movements of flailing arms and a hand grasping tight to what she discerns is a Gatekeeper's invitation.

"You have an invitation! Congratulations!" She is happy for the disgruntled weaver. But he will not be cheered.

"You think that, do you? Humph! I've waited a long time for this, thinking it would have more to offer than just ONE word. Useless to me." Arms fling wildly in the air again. "Just useless."

Perplexed, Weaver asks, "Well, what does it say? What does it invite you to?"

"Not what I expected, that's for sure." The word weaver with the invitation grumbles again. "I can't commit myself to something so risky. Just not enough here for me to put it all out there on the line. It's not worth it, I tell you. It's just not worth it."

The inconsolable nature of this fellow's declarations impose a wall of much ado. Weaver shrinks from venturing forward with any threads of encouragement. Her curiosity piques, though, for she has never seen a Gatekeeper's invitation with her own eyes up close. She doesn't know what the protocol to receive an invitation could be—only the requirements that everyone knows, as etched on the gateway signpost for all to see.

An awkward silence surrounds them as they stand together, and Weaver can think of no other response than to quietly say, "I'm sorry."

The angry word-weaver glares at her, then at the Gatekeeper across the square. Shaking his head and rolling his eyes in disgust, he flings the invitation into Weaver's hands and growls. "Here then. You take it. No use to you, either, I'm sure."

And he is gone. Stomping away from the market square, down a side street off Waiting Lane, into the darkness.

Weaver stands alone, the invitation in her hand, frozen with indecision. What an unexpected stroke this is!

Five minutes or more pass—perhaps a mere ten seconds. Weaver surveys the blank envelope, torn open with hope and vigor, only to disappoint. She looks at the back of a folded card, also blank, with no markings on the outside at all. On the inside, one word. What could it be? Dare she peek? The much-desired invitation to take possession of the Gatekeeper's key and unlock the gate into opportunity on the other side is in Weaver's hands.

But someone is watching. She feels probing eyes. A sense of guilt washes over her. This is not her invitation. It belongs to another weaver. One who did not take advantage of it and despised its worth. One who gave it away. Does she have the right to own it? Should she return it to the Gatekeeper?

Weaver looks toward the gate and sees him—the Gatekeeper—his eyes scrutinizing her. He sees that she is holding an invitation. An invitation he has not given her. Convicted in her heart, she resolves to return it to the Gatekeeper immediately.

His stern expression appears tempered by a flush of tenderness in his eyes as she draws near to him, slipping from the safe shadows into the light of the open courtyard. She thinks herself suddenly very brave for doing this noble thing. Perhaps, she will weave a tale about it when she returns home, and tuck it away with so many other records of her life experiences.

"You there!" the Gatekeeper calls to her with command. "Where did you get that invitation?"

Dumbstruck at being addressed, Weaver owns her answer. "It was given to me by another weaver. He didn't want it. I'm returning it to you, sir. It's not mine, I know."

A warmth in the Gatekeeper's eyes invites her to smile as she stretches out her hand to give him the invitation. "You did not read it?" he says.

"No, sir."

"But you had the opportunity to do so. Why did you not seize it?"

The Gatekeeper's question surprises her. Here she is, displaying a nobility of character to return the invitation that is not hers, and the Gatekeeper seems disappointed in her virtuous act. "I . . . I . . . I was not given the invitation. It belongs to someone else."

The Gatekeeper's eyes narrow. He leans forward, speaking slowly. "Don't you want to be invited into the Field of Dreams? Don't you want to have the opportunity to realize your full potential as a weaver of words? Don't you want to own the key that unlocks this gate to possess all those things for yourself?"

The questions thunder in her heart. Potential! Opportunity! Her Field of Dreams! These things, long desired by her, wait beyond the gate. The Gatekeeper has the key. Here she stands face to face with him, challenged to lay hold of it all. Is he testing her?

In that instant, she glances behind him to the etching on the gate: *Prove purpose to me, that you know your calling, for only the called gain the key.* Weaver's words tumble from her lips before her reason reins them in. "I have desired the Key of Opportunity ever since I can remember! Weaving is my life. It is breath to me. If I could not do it, I could do nothing else."

Clamping her mouth shut, she presses her lips together so as not to leak any more revelations of her heart.

The Gatekeeper lifts an eyebrow, regarding her with amusement. She wonders if he is making fun of her; humoring her, perhaps. Why didn't he just take the invitation back? She has done the honorable thing to return it.

"You know," muses the Gatekeeper as he slips his thumbs through his belt loops. He taps his aged fingers on the key by his side. "You appear somewhat confused. Your words say one thing, but your actions prove another."

Weaver does not respond. She is confused. The Gatekeeper continues. "What is that tapestry you're clinging to there? May I see it?"

Weaver steals swift, furtive glances to her left and her right. Is the Gatekeeper addressing someone else? No. Everyone has left the square. Only the Gatekeeper and Weaver remain.

"May I see your tapestry?" the Gatekeeper inquires again, holding his hand out toward her.

"It's my tapestry. My latest work. A story I've woven with many intricate patterns, using quality threads and yarns." She opens the tapestry before the Gatekeeper. He lowers his head to study the work as she notes more words on the signpost behind him: *Display your passion in what you produce; a product I have to see.*

Silently, Weaver waits while the Gatekeeper reviews her work, swaying anxiously in anticipation.

How did this moment arrive? An instant earlier, she cowered on the sidelines with her hopes and dreams. Now—could this be truly happening? She stands face to face in audience with the Gatekeeper—a Master Story-Weaver. He diligently examines her craftsmanship even though she hadn't been given an invitation!

Or, had she.

Her right hand still held the cast-off invitation tight between her fingers. The Gatekeeper did not show an interest in having it returned to him. In fact, he directly challenged her to prove her Purpose and Product as a weaver of words. Isn't that what happens to those who receive an invitation? This mysterious invitation with only one word on it is offensive enough for at least one word-weaver to have tossed it away as worthless. Now it is in her possession. This presents her with an opportunity. And, a choice.

The Gatekeeper looks up from his examination. "You have an invitation, do you not?"

Weaver looks at the envelope and card in her hand. She makes a choice. "Yes." she answers plainly.

"But, you have not read it?"

"No." Weaver stammers. "I . . . I didn't think I could. It wasn't mine to read."

"So then, you don't want to read it? You don't want to know what's written there? You don't want an invitation?"

"Yes. Yes, I do!" Weaver realizes she has passed the point of no return. This moment of opportunity, of invitation, of audience with a Master Story-Weaver and Gatekeeper, may never come for her again.

"Then," grins the Gatekeeper, "Read the invitation and follow the direction."

Slowly, Weaver lifts the card to her view and opens it. There, in golden letters threaded with electricity, energized, as though leaping from the page, she reads the one word: "GO." She remembers the disgruntled word-weaver who had the invitation, but chose not to "go." He expected more. He must have thought there would be detailed instructions. More provision. More than just a command to "go" with no specific promises.

But, Keys of Opportunity don't work that way. Opportunity requires response. Opportunity demands to be seized. To be wrestled with. To be faced fearlessly and held fast to the finish. Opportunity expects one to "go" and not to flee, nor shrink back in trepidation.

Weaver's eyes focus on the third requirement etched upon the gate: *Persevere—show fearless effort; face your foes to the finish; persevere in the fray; do not flee.*

In that moment, she realizes that she is on the threshold of her Field of Dreams. Through serendipitous means she is a breath away from a new chapter in her story tapestry. How will she respond in this watershed moment? Words to the purpose must not fail her now.

A glint of light distracts her muse. The Gatekeeper dangles the Key of Opportunity before Weaver, bidding her response. Will she . . . GO?

Journal and Discuss

The Gatekeeper's Key is an allegory using figurative language. This means that elements in the story have hidden meanings illustrating a principle or truth like the parables that Jesus told. Review this list of metaphorical terms from the story. What more can you find in the story? Add them to this list.

- Wannabe Village
- Muchado Wall
- Gateway to Greater Things
- Field of Dreams
- Gatekeeper
- Waiting Lane
- Key of Opportunity
- Tapestry
- Mistress Doubts-A-Lot
- Seed
- Invitation
- Key

Define the metaphorical terms listed as they relate to you, or to some of the terms defined in the Appendix. Break each one down as to how you might personally apply the metaphors in the story. For instance, make these generalized terms specific to yourself:

- Muchado Wall = Obstacles to reaching a desired goal
- Waiting Lane = A desert season in your life
- Tapestry = A personal goal, ministry, health, etc.
- Field of Dreams = Answered prayer
- Key = The thing required before receiving desire

 Thoughtfully explore who you might be were you to live in Wannabe Village. Weaver is clearly a writer. If you are not a writer, determine who you are by defining what makes up your Field of Dreams. Who are the mentor Gatekeepers holding the Key of Opportunity in your life? Who can help you to cross the threshold through the Gateway of Greater Things?

 Define your Purpose, your Product, and what you must do to Persevere to reach your Field of Dreams.

Sometimes the Gateway of Greater Things requires more than one key to unlock its portal. In the following essays, we'll explore what some of those keys are and what must be done to possess them when the Gatekeeper of your soul invites you to cross thresholds in your life, calling you to grow into greater things. You'll be challenged at the end of each chapter with questions relating Weaver's story in *The Gatekeeper's Key*, to other characters in some of my favorite literary classics, plus personal experience journal excerpts.

Have you received an invitation from a Gatekeeper?

Are you seeking a Gatekeeper's Key?

Will you GO?

~ The Gatekeeper's Key: Chapter 2—The Key of Love ~

There are times when you cannot understand
why you cannot do what you want to do.
When God brings the blank space,
see that you do not fill it in, but wait.

Oswald Chambers

Chapter 2: The Key of Love
In Waiting, Know Patience

I wait for the Lord, my soul waits,
And in His word I do hope.
My soul waits for the Lord
More than those who watch for the morning—
Yes, more than those who watch for the morning.

Psalm 130:5-6 NKJV

Miss Bertram longs to pass through a locked gate:

> *Yes, certainly the sun shines and the park looks very cheerful, but unluckily that iron gate . . . gives me a feeling of restraint and hardship. I cannot get out, as the starling said . . .*

Jane Austen
Chapter 10, *Mansfield Park*

Mansfield Park is a celebrated novel by Jane Austen, written in the spirit of a cautionary tale. Its memorable characters wrestle through a plot peppered with a host of powerful passages, witty turn of phrases, and sharp insights on the human condition.

By this scene in chapter ten, as quoted above, the aristocratic Miss Bertram has become disenchanted with her fiancé, Mr. Rushworth. He accompanies her on a walk through the grounds of his estate where she is soon to be mistress. A third member of their party is a newcomer to the neighborhood named Mr. Crawford—a carefree cad, captivating young hearts with his provocative manner. Miss Bertram, quite swept away with his charms, flirts into the clutch of his temptations, imprisoning herself in both jealousy, regret, and discontent. Dangerous territory. She is, after all, in the throes of planning her wedding to another.

Arriving at the threshold of an expanded meadow in the sprawling park, they cannot pass through the locked gate.

Here, a powerful metaphor illustrates Miss Bertram's fettered heart as she complains, "I cannot get out." She feels like a victim, imprisoned through the cause of others. Trapped. Unconscious of the guilt of her own heart on the verge of betrayal and scandal.

Her outcry is a literary allusion to a line from a late 18th century novel titled, *A Sentimental Journey*. The words, "I cannot get out, as the starling said," recall an imprisoned starling in the Bastille at the outset of the French Revolution. Though set free from a metal cage, he remains in a tower prison. He sees beyond an iron trellis to freedom, but cannot pass through it to liberation, and laments, "I cannot get out. I cannot get out."

Living life trapped behind a trellised window with all the glories of a heart's desire within view, but beyond reach, feeds discontentment to the soul. Jane's metaphor brilliantly exposes this aspect of Miss Bertram's character. She, like the starling, laments feeling a prisoner on this side of a locked gate. Such has been a common complaint in humans from the time of Adam and Eve. The consequence of their sin imprisoned them and all their descendants to life on the down side of the Garden Gate.

Miss Bertram expresses a wish of passing through the locked gate into the more promising park beyond, that . . .

> *". . . their views and their plans might be more comprehensive. It was the very thing of all others to be wished, it was the best, it was the only way of proceeding with any advantage . . . Go therefore they must to that knoll, and through that gate; but the gate was locked."*

Though quite determined, Miss Bertram settles for less. But. For. The. Key.

> *"Mr. Rushworth wished he had brought the key; he had been very near thinking whether he should not bring the key; he was determined he would never come without the key again, but still this did not remove the present evil. They could not get through; and as Miss Bertram's inclination for so doing did by no means lessen, it ended in Mr. Rushworth's declaring outright that he would go and fetch the key. He set off accordingly."*

If you're an Austen fan of *Mansfield Park*, you'll remember Mr. Rushworth stops, turns around, and heroically goes in the opposite direction to get the key, quite repenting of his carelessness in leaving it behind. Unfortunately, he leaves Miss Bertram behind in the bad company of the unsavory Mr. Crawford. She could not do what she wished at the time she wished it—a blank space. Mr. Crawford fills the void of Mr. Rushworth, urging her to not wait for the key, but to squeeze through the gate to the park beyond, achieving her desires by another way.

Most inappropriate.

Neither Mr. Crawford nor Miss Bertram meet with a desirable end in the story, I'm afraid. The inevitable consequences of their poor choices are quite in keeping with a want of virtuous character on both their parts. Alas! They are doomed to reject redemption. They really ought to have waited for the key, because, you see—there was one.

A Key.

That thing uniquely designed to open the locked gate, making a way so "their views and their plans might be more comprehensive." So they might see all things perfectly.

> *Now, we see things imperfectly, like puzzling reflections in a mirror, but then we will see everything with perfect clarity. All that I know now is partial and incomplete, but then I will know everything completely, just as God now knows me completely."*
> 1 Corinthians 13:12 NLT

I often think of this scene when tempted to take another way to making my views and plans more comprehensive, complete, and fulfilled, but for some blockage barring my way. Like a locked iron gate.

Waiting on the downside of an obstruction, with the promise of the glories beyond in my line of sight, tempts me to devise alternative methods to reach my goals. The key to properly unlock and open the way before me is slow in coming. Surely, there must be another way because—I WANT IT NOW!

Paul addressed this in his first letter to the Corinthians who begin well enough. They take the Key of Faith and set themselves on the foundation of Christ through salvation. Subsequently, they come to possess the Key of Hope, bringing them to the threshold of a vast parkland alive with God's promises.

The Corinthian believers eagerly sought to take full possession of what God promised them, though they pursued His gifts imperfectly. Chaotically, in fact. Paul affirms their desire to possess all God's best gifts, but rebukes their inappropriate methods of acting on their zeal.

You see, in practice they tried to squeeze through the locked gate with the small space afforded them holding only two keys, when in fact, a third key was necessary to unlock and swing wide the gate.

> *Three things will last forever—faith, hope, and love. And the greatest of these is love.*
>
> 1 Corinthians 13:13 NLT

The Key of Love

There's a melody, like the starling's bird-song, that plays out of tune in our world today. It begins within our own discontented hearts. There's no use pointing fingers assuming our sour notes are the fault of others. The truth finds us out. Zealously we charge forward, unwilling to wait for our Love who has promised to bring us the Key of Love. The key that makes complete.

In the waiting comes completeness. In trying times of trial, patience refines the motives of our heart. Perfected, the key turns the lock of a balanced three-part harmony in our life-song: Faith, Hope, and Love

God is Love. He is worthy of the wait.

But, waiting is hard. Waiting on the Lord to unlock the gate so we might cross the threshold into the fullness of His calling and the thing we most desire is hardest of all. We have prayed to such an end for so very long. Holding fast on this side of the gate . . . waiting in a blank space. It seems like a great waste of time when we could be about the business of doing and being. Of walking in answered prayer for healing, provision, fulfillment.

But, what grace—what love—the boundaries of a locked gate can be in our lives, were we to regard it as a gift, rather than an impediment! Far too often, when things don't pan out in the way and the time we desire, we divine our own answers to our prayers. Sometimes we rush ahead of God, outside of His ordered steps. Our motivation in seeking our ends skews. We dethrone the perfect will of God for a will of our own devising.

There is a thin line between advancing in ordained initiative and asserting in self-will. Brokenness may result from both. Developing patience in waiting seasons brings one to the threshold of brokenness in the trying of our character when dreams delay. Or detour.

But in God's economy, this is a good thing. Brokenness forces us to make way for a new thing—a life molded and tested in the fires of waiting. On Him. As with a bride and groom anticipating their wedding day through the months of betrothal and promise until fulfilled, God uses the blank spaces of waiting, in patience, as a time of preparation rather than loss of purpose or precious desires.

Truly, more is accomplished during this time in secret chambers than is readily visible. Consider a chick hidden inside the shell of an egg, incubating. God does not intend for it to remain there indefinitely. The womb opens, producing its fruit in due season.

> *We are like eggs at present. And you cannot go on indefinitely being just an ordinary, decent egg. We must be hatched or go bad.*
> C. S. Lewis

God does not intend for us to "go bad." The promise of His faithful love to birth good things and beauty in our lives is resident in the waiting time. While she lingered in her blank space by the locked iron gate, Miss Bertram's betrothed was engaged in the business of meeting the desire of her heart to pass through the gate into the promising gardens beyond. In her waiting lived her hope. She did not have the key to the gate, but she did possess the Key of Love, had she the heart to use it. But her blank space blinded her.

Waiting on the perceived missing link between where we are now and where we hope to be, can try our patience and weary the soul to the place of brokenness. Holding fast to the Key of Love—God's Love—in such times allows our eyes to see His busy on our behalf in the secret chambers of our heart. In seeing thus, patience is no longer tested, but developed. A weary soul grows stronger, and only the bits of self that ought to be broken off break away. And are swept away. This makes room for Patience to fill the void, Peace to move in, and Contentment to complete the picture.

Should this be the case, living on Waiting Lane is a productive time, indeed. Standing fast and faithful on the threshold of a locked iron gate in the sure hope of the soon return of a lover finds its eventual reward.

In truth, all waiting is waiting on God when you know God—when you are convinced of His goodness and purposes in your life to move your forward into better. Into His best.

It is the Key of Love that unlocks such riches in our character. Thankfully, Paul gives us a detailed look at how our Faith and Hope should be walked out in the practical of true Love. The motives of our heart must be fit:

> *If I could speak all the languages of earth and of angels, but didn't love others, I would only be a noisy gong or a clanging cymbal. If I had the gift of prophecy, and if I understood all of God's secret plans and possessed all knowledge, and if I had such faith that I could move mountains, but didn't love others, I would be nothing. If I gave everything I have*

> *to the poor and even sacrificed my body, I could boast about it; but if I didn't love others, I would have gained nothing. Love is patient and kind. Love is not jealous or boastful or proud or rude. It does not demand its own way. It is not irritable, and it keeps no record of being wronged. It does not rejoice about injustice but rejoices whenever the truth wins out. Love never gives up, never loses faith, is always hopeful, and endures through every circumstance.*
>
> 1 Corinthians 13:1-7 NLT

Are you lingering in the shadows on Waiting Lane wondering why a locked gate stands between you and God's calling and promises on the other side? Is it a ministry you have a passion to walk in or a specific answer to prayer for healing, a job, relationship, deliverance, and provision you are seeking? Are you zealous to possess the prize before you've taken the ordered steps to achieve it?

Your Love is on His way to you with the Key to unlock the gate. Will you wait, trusting that you will cross the threshold to all the good things and beauty reserved for you at the appointed time? Provision in place? All things in order? Heart motives pure?

If only Miss Bertram had put her Faith and Hope in her betrothed Love, waiting on him for the key to the gate! Instead, she allowed herself distraction and discontentment through the machinations of an evil outsider. He aimed only to exploit her weaknesses and exult himself. Mr. Crawford was quite the villain of the piece, to be sure.

Indeed, Jane Austen gives us a cautionary tale here, mirroring profound biblical principles. When story implants God's Word deep into our hearts, our soul motives are exposed. We recognize the reality of ourselves in the person of a fictional character. Should we learn well the lesson, we might change Miss Bertram's lament to a love song, chirping with delight in joyful tones:

> "I cannot get GOD out . . . I cannot get GOD out . . .
> as the starling said . . ."

Journal and Discuss

Regarding C. S. Lewis' illustration of an egg that must be hatched and its relation to developing patience in waiting seasons: How is being in a place of incubation—waiting—a place of anticipation and expectant hope? Within our eggshells of provision and protection, the life principles of growth, increase, maturation, and development take place. Incubation within a shell, for a season, is absolutely necessary for the preparation to cross barriers into greater things. How we perceive our provision and protection in our time of incubation determines how we will come to the end of that season. But, egg incubator seasons often feel like being stuck in a rut. Don't let the darkness blind you to God's secret work as He cultivates your spirit to His likeness.

What are you waiting on the Lord for? What broken bits in your heart must you sweep away for patience to grow? What practical things can you do while you wait on your Beloved to come to you with the key to unlock the gate? How can you make the waiting seasons of incubation in your life a time of vision and hope?

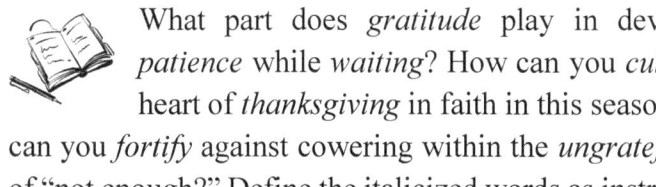
What part does *gratitude* play in developing *patience* while *waiting*? How can you *cultivate* a heart of *thanksgiving* in faith in this season? How can you *fortify* against cowering within the *ungrateful* shell of "not enough?" Define the italicized words as instructed in the Word Study Appendix using *Webster's 1828 Dictionary*.

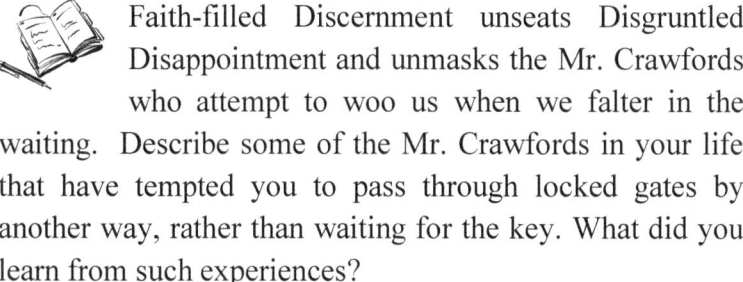
Faith-filled Discernment unseats Disgruntled Disappointment and unmasks the Mr. Crawfords who attempt to woo us when we falter in the waiting. Describe some of the Mr. Crawfords in your life that have tempted you to pass through locked gates by another way, rather than waiting for the key. What did you learn from such experiences?

Compare Weaver's shrinking back, lingering in the shadows of Waiting Lane, too fearful to step out nearer the gate, to Miss Bertram rushing forth to breach the gate by any means. Which character shows more discernment? That may be a trick question. Why? One of the most frustrating things about waiting times in our lives is discerning when the time of waiting is ended. Sometimes the gates in our lives unlock and swing wide open so that there is no doubt we ought to cross thresholds and expand our borders. Other times, the gate simply unlocks and it is for us to know we ought to push it open and advance. In such times, how can we be sure of how we are to act?

~ The Gatekeeper's Key: Chapter 3—The Key of Courage ~

Thou hast only to follow the wall far enough and there will be a door in it.

Brother Luke

Chapter 3: The Key of Courage
In Acceptance, Embrace Confidence

I know thy works. Behold I have set before thee an open door and no man shall shut it: For thou hast a little strength and hast not denied my Name.
Revelations 3:8 KJV

*Do not be afraid of sudden terror,
Nor of trouble from the wicked when it comes;
For the Lord will be your confidence,
And will keep your foot from being caught.*
Proverbs 3:25-26 NKJV

I embraced my calling with certainty. The passion to pursue writing and speaking through storytelling and the creative arts burned deep within me from my youth. I loved the stage. Acting out stories. Taking the things I learned about life and creating tangible representations of intangible truths. I found the crack in the mortar of Muchado Wall at an early age and peeked through it to a Field of Dreams beyond. A seed rooted, locked in place, and has cultivated in my heart ever since.

As an adult, I came to know the Lord as He who held for me the Key of Love. What grew from that dream-seed required significant pruning. Jesus, the Husbandman of my soul, deftly cut away the wild vines fallen in the mud and lifted others up, tying them in place to prosper with a new view of the sun. His life-giving perspective sprouted and matured within me as He trained mind and heart to blossom in a biblical worldview.

Now, I had something to write about! I desired to direct others to God as Savior and Lover of souls for divine purposes through my words. My love of learning and literature put me in church ministry, Christian classrooms, and homeschool venues discipling families. God also opened doors within the community and public school environments to shine like a star, lighting the way to know Him. I grew steadily, seeking Gatekeepers along the way to mentor me towards excellence in my field.

Through deep valleys, level plains, high mountains, parched lands, and fragrant fields, as a journeyman I proved my calling across the borders and landmarks of God's Word and world. Seasons of plenty and want disciplined my craft as it matured my spirit. Trials weighed on the balance with blessings—both gifts for my well-being. Marriage, children, multiple moves, loss of loved ones, divorce, remarriage, and grandchildren performed their appointed task on the stage of my life. Each scene in the play molded me into the character of Christ. Gatekeepers invited me with the necessary keys to open gates, iron entryways, wooden doors, and stage curtains, at the appointed times.

But, even with such a resume, the Field of Dreams remained elusive. Just beyond reach, it seemed. Not quite in my grasp. Ever and always I was on the path to arrival, yet never arriving. Always a journeyman, never the master.

Then, quite unexpectedly, a new door opened with an invitation to mastery. Confidently, I accepted a dream job when offered to me in a secular venue. Name my own price, they said. Choose my own hours. Teach whatever I like, they promised. My years of hard work appeared to pay off. My creativity and reputation preceded me and my unique experience in drama and creative communications would make the arts program at their school a magnet for growth and enrollment. I was to be the master in this new work. I leapt at the opportunity to be starlight for Christ in a dark place. It was everything I could have hoped for—and more.

But, within three years, I found myself undone, paralyzed in a prison of broken promises, working within a corrupt system seeking to remake me into their image. My light snuffed by darkness. I questioned everything I'd ever learned about my calling, craft, and philosophy of education. Waiting for rescue, I feared that I'd been run too far off the rails with no hope of arriving at Destiny Station.

When at last, the day came, and I was unceremoniously dumped from my position, I wallowed at home crumpled in fear, paralyzed by failure, and crushed in confusion. Out of a job with no clear path forward, using little strength I cried unto the Lord in a prayerful sonnet . . .

> *Failing into the arms of God,*
> *My salvation is His Grace.*
> *Bouncing back in abounding joy,*
> *Empowered to run the race.*
> *"Make mine weak," the winner says,*
> *"I much prefer its taste!"*

> *In gratitude, I hydrate thus,*
> *In failure is no waste.*
> *Greater than I will make feet fleet*
> *The miraculous with each stride.*
> *A carefree brow knows no sweat*
> *Clinging to Christ for the ride.*
>
> > *Thus I will ever in faith run,*
> > *Til all His promises I have won.*

In my petition to the Divine Gatekeeper, a new invitation arrived on the threshold of my heart. One word only, defined from *Noah Webster's 1828 Dictionary* (see Appendix for word study details): Constellation.

CONSTELLATION:
1. A cluster of fixed stars
2. An assemblage of splendors or excellencies

I did what I knew to do with a word when it came my way. I studied it. First, "constellation," and then the key words within its definition. In this case, two:

FIXED: Settled; established; firm; fast; stable.

STAR:
> An apparently small luminous body in the heavens, that appears in the night . . . Stars are fixed or planetary. The fixed stars are known by their perpetual twinkling, and by their being always in the same position in relation to each other. The planets do not twinkle, and they revolve about the sun. The stars are worlds, and their immense numbers exhibit the astonishing extent of creation and of divine power.

In addition, the Noah *Webster's 1828 Dictionary of the English Language* further notes that:

> In Scripture, Christ is called the bright and morning star the star that ushers in the light of an eternal day to his people. *Revelations 22.*

> Ministers are also called stars in Christ's right hand, as, being supported and directed by Christ, they convey light and knowledge to the followers of Christ. *Revelations 1.*

My Field of Dreams suddenly expanded onto a landscape of night sky. We only see stars when it is dark, you know. Two key Scriptures relate to stars and constellations:

> *He also made the stars. God set these lights in the sky to light the earth, to govern the day and night, and to separate the light from the darkness.*
> Genesis 1:16-18 NLT

> *Those who are wise will shine as bright as the sky, and those who will shine like the stars forever lead many to righteousness.*
> Daniel 12:3 NLT

A star-studded key materialized in my hand. The calling to courageously pick myself up off the muddy ground and tie up my vines to branch out into new growth, brought me to the threshold of a new gateway to God's purposes. Though I felt like my legs had been cut from under me, still the Lord called me to press on—even if all I could do was limp. I looked for the Gatekeeper, and it was to be ME.

So began a serpentine route to where I am today: developing a ministry of writing, speaking, and storytelling as tools for teaching and learning to equip homeschool and Christian families in prioritizing a Family Literacy Lifestyle as the primary educators and disciplers of their children.

Like a constellation, a "cluster" of young moms seeking guidance and support in their homeschool efforts teamed with me to launch Constellation Academy Homeschool Resources Network. Together we learned to shine brightly as "an assemblage of splendors or excellencies," in each other's lives to support each of our collective families, and academic goals. My children's homeschool days were long gone, yet my home was once again a schoolhouse.

Which brought me to a door in the wall with courageous steps on wobbly legs, rewarded.

I conducted afternoon classes with students that first year. My junior high class enjoyed a medieval history class along with a literature study of Marguerite de Angeli's Newbery Award Winning Book, *The Door in the Wall*. It perfectly captured in fiction, what I'd just lived in real life.

A Door in the Wall

It is a critical time in young Robin's life, left paralyzed and unable to walk, from a strange sickness. Both his parents are away. He is overcome with despair and the dashed dreams of one day following in the footsteps of his father as a knight of the realm. He watches all his friends go off to take their position as pages in the castles of great knights. He, too, had received an invitation to serve, and was scheduled to leave home and fulfill the destiny of a highborn son.

Instead, the walls of his room and the confines of a sick bed imprison him. The void of a great blank space spreads before him, foreshadowing his future. The servants desert him, for fear of the plague. He lies abandoned and alone.

Until Brother Luke arrives—a Gatekeeper—at an opportune, providential moment.

He brings with him an invitation to advance forward to a place of healing and the eventual transport to the destiny prepared for him. But Robin's dire condition is all he knows. Surely, he will always be too weak and too small to contribute anything of value in the world. Traveling to hospital and then onto a life of destiny and purpose is unlikely now. He complains, a victim of gross injustice, pointing out a myriad of impossibilities to the plan.

> *"But I cannot walk," said Robin woefully. "See you, my two legs are as useless as if they were logs of wood. How shall I go there? My father is with the King at the Scottish wars, and with him are all his men at arms. My lady mother has been commanded to attend upon Her Majesty the Queen. It is supposed by them that I am now page in the household of Sir Peter de Lindsay at his castle in the north."*

To be sure, great calamity fell upon the innocent, unexpected and in a very short span of time. Trauma blinds even the heartiest for a season. But Brother Luke, the wise Gatekeeper that he is, opens the eyes of Robin's understanding that he might find courage and accept the call to go forth regardless of his limitations:

> *"Dost remember the long wall that is about the garden of thy father's house?"*
>
> *"Yes," said Robin, "of course. Why?"*
>
> *"Dost remember, too, the wall about the Tower or any other wall?" Robin nodded. "Have they not all a door somewhere?"*
>
> *"Yes," said Robin again.*
>
> *Always remember that," said the friar, "Thou hast only to follow the wall far enough and there will be a door in it."*

Indeed, traveling in medieval times is fraught with difficulty and danger—and a great many walls. The friar takes young Robin under his wing, committed to watching over him on the long journey to Sir Peter's castle.

The lad, overwhelmed with anger and despair at the loss of his legs, and his broken dream of one day becoming a knight, kicks against the goads of his mentor. Patiently, Brother Luke breaks his will to save his spirit, through a series of trials and required disciplines. The rigors of Robin's circumstances and daily ministrations of the friar eventually bolster him with new hope, buoy him with confidence, and ready him for his journey to Sir Peter's castle. Whatever destiny lies ahead there for him, he does not know. But he has learned contentment in whatever will be.

~ The Gatekeeper's Key: Chapter 3—The Key of Courage ~

Along the way, villainy grips the town they travel through and they find themselves prisoners under siege, surrounded by enemy soldiers. Robin musters the courage to escape alone, through a literal secret door in the wall, to seek aid. His handicap as a cripple suits him now as strong armor, useful to deceive the foe. If soldiers discover him, he will not be perceived as a threat. Now, Robin must become the Gatekeeper to open the way of rescue for an entire town!

Boldly, he hobbles on his crutches, unhindered, crossing the threshold of the enemy lines. Courage empowers clever means to fool the enemy, and he makes his way to Sir Peter's castle, achieving his goal to summon help and save the day.

Walls, fences, and locked gates appear at every turn on Robin's journey from sick bed to success, acting as shepherds directing him onto providential pathways. In every test of patience or encounter of peril, a door in the wall opens, revealing many Gatekeepers with keys en route, and bold invitations to go forward. Ever forward.

Then one day, he becomes the Gatekeeper, caretaker of the key, making a way of passage through siege walls for those he loves.

Sometimes we must accept the invitation—the challenge—to limp our way through unorthodox gates in unstable seasons, becoming the unlikely hero in our story. Gatekeepers who equip us with the Key of Courage in such times, unlock confidence to advance us boldly where we must go, but never thought we could.

As I mentored my handful of homeschoolers through this literature study, I saw my own situation within the drama. What did the master learn?

Courage and confidence never come our way until we are willing to accept and embrace our life circumstances.

I've always felt like I've been stumbling about, gimpy-legged, from one thing to another. Never positioned long enough to build walls around staked property. Setting limits. When territory I thought was mine had to be relinquished, I lost my bearings.

Clutching what you think is the fulfillment of your dream too tightly can morph into a nightmare. Discouragement results. Confidence is unseated. This becomes a wall impossible to breach apart from resilience and wise Gatekeepers. But, *"Thou hast only to follow the wall far enough and there will be a door in it."*

Constellation Academy became my door in the wall. It opened my life and put my fumbling feet onto a far better track to advance me nearer my Field of Dreams, calling me forward. Ever forward.

In fact, I would not be writing and publishing today had I remained in that high-paying secular school job. Like me, Robin's life path dramatically changed. But his calling to serve others in a customized Field of Dreams only altered in structure, not substance. Sir Peter reminds him that destiny is always ours, though it may transform in the journey to living it out fully and complete.

"Each of us has his place in the world . . . if we can not serve in one way, there is always another. If we do what we are able, a door always opens to something else."

Sir Peter de Lindsay

When coming to the threshold of crisis, accept your circumstances and embrace confidence. Walk, limp, stumble, and run the race with the Key of Courage to finish.

Journal and Discuss

Robin's envy of his friends leaving home to begin their journey to knighthood while he remained confined to his bed is similar to Weaver's envy of the other word weavers receiving invitations from the Gatekeeper, and she not. Discuss how they are similar and how they differ. What happened in each of their characters to move them beyond that limitation in their lives?

Calling. Courage. Confidence. Acceptance. Embrace. These, and others are worthy of a word study. Use the online *Noah Webster's 1828 Dictionary* tool at webstersdictionary1828.com to complete a word study on each as instructed in the Appendix.

How many of your dreams became nightmares and you woke, ready to dream anew? How many comfort zones became intolerably confining, forcing you to break free and grow into greater things?

~ The Gatekeeper's Key: Chapter 4—The Key of Faith ~

The pursuit of calling—a grace mastered one trusting leap of faith at a time.

Kathryn Ross

Chapter 4: The Key of Faith
In Trust, Commit Obedience

*Now faith is the substance of things hoped for,
the evidence of things not seen.*
                                    Hebrews 11:1 NKJV

*By faith Abraham obeyed when he was called to go out to
the place which he would receive as an inheritance.
And he went out, not knowing where he was going.*
                                    Hebrews 11:8 NKJV

*The Lord God is my strength, and He will make my feet
like Hinds' feet, and He will make me to walk
upon mine High Places.*
                                    Habakkuk 3:19 KJV

Years ago, as a young Navy wife, our family moved for a two-year tour of duty to Idaho Falls, Idaho. We planned a four-day cross-country trip with two toddlers, two cars, and a cat. According to the map in those pre-GPS days (the old-fashioned fold out state maps—one for each state between South Carolina and Idaho), our destination was just on the other side of the Grand Teton Mountain Range. I was familiar enough with the mountainous areas along the eastern parts of the country, but soon learned it was folly to judge the mountains of the great Northwest by the same yardstick. There is no comparison.

Seeing the Grand Tetons from a distance, I believed we were only a couple of hours away from our new home. Enjoying the ride at the outset, the tall, pointed peak soaring high ahead bore little resemblance to the mountains of my limited acquaintance. As the car climbed to loftier heights, I anticipated a great valley on the other side where I expected the land to flatten out and our journey end.

Boy, did I get that wrong!

Just as we reached the crest of one mountain, two more loomed into view, eerily crowned by low-hanging clouds. The thick haze blocked further vision, blinding my ability to see any more of what may lie ahead. With a deep breath of resolve, I soldiered on. Surely, the end of the line would be just around the bend of *this* mountain.

But, alas! Yet another three taller peaks jutted high before me. There was nothing for it. I pressed on for the prize of the other side.

As morning wore into afternoon and the hours lapsed away, I had yet to see an end in sight. Discouragement crept into my moving car as Hopelessness enveloped me. I wondered if we'd taken the wrong road. Surely there was a better route through these mountains. Something that wouldn't take so very long. A back-way to cut out the endless up and down and over and around at higher and higher altitudes.

However, this proved to be mere wishful thinking. The map was very clear, affirming there to be only one way—and this was it. The charted course plotted the direction I was

~ The Gatekeeper's Key: Chapter 4—The Key of Faith ~

to take and would brook no remonstrance. Obedience was my singular option.

I forced myself to be the grown-up. No melt-downs. No impatient tantrums because things weren't happening fast enough to suit me. No. This was the way and I was to walk in it. No turning back.

> Trust the map
> Obey the road signs;
> Faithful in season,
> Follow God's Guidelines.

During that long, long day, I fought fatigue and battled boredom. Beautiful as the mountains were, after so many hours the scenery blended into one great froth of fog, pine trees, and jagged peaks, sharp and linear like rows of shark teeth, threatening.

I feared I might fall asleep at the wheel and plunge over the cliff's edge towards destruction in a valley below. The promise of reaching a climax up and over one mountain left me with the trial of yet another apex to conquer. And, another. And another.

This was not a road trip for the faint of heart. Even so, the car had a full tank of gas and was thoroughly prepared for the mountain climbing job when we'd left that morning on this last leg of our journey. I, however, was running low on faith fuel, confined as I was in a car for so long. And weary. A filling station of fortitude to the task was in order, but I hadn't seen anything to break the monotony of the mountains for hours that would give hope.

In truth, after the novelty of the first few mountain summits wore off, I felt like giving up. I thought I'd never see flatlands again. I wanted to find the first rest stop, call Mommy, have her send a helicopter, pluck me out of this cross-country madness, and send me back home. Kids, cat, and what-all. I didn't want to move in the first place!

The digital clock in the car dashboard clicked the hours away. Tick. Tick. Tick

What a treasure the gift of Time is! God gives us ample in each season. Sometimes, we think it too much—sometimes too little. But, in the end . . . there is an end.

The map clearly showed there was another side of this mountain range. Each mile, each moment, ticked closer to the reward of an end. Here was a thing, faithful and true, to which I could cling.

One consolation, as the dreary hours passed, was a fertile imagination fed by reading. Books. Stories. And one in particular came to mind with every twist and turn of the mountain pathway: *Hinds Feet in High Places*, by Hannah Hurnard. The subtitle on the cover of my well-worn copy read: *An allegory dramatizing the journey each of us must take before we can live in "high places."*

I might have been the heroine, Much Afraid, in that story. She receives an invitation from the Chief Shepherd to follow Him to the high places where he would make her wobbly legs strong to leap like hinds over rocky terrain. His wooing captivated her heart and soul, but living in the Valley of Humiliation with her gruesome relatives, the Family of Fearing, she thought herself unworthy to accept an invitation—even though such a call came with the key to the desires of her heart: to live in the Kingdom of Love.

> *[But, she said,] "How is that possible? And what would the inhabitants of the Kingdom of Love say to the presence of a wretched little cripple with an ugly face and a twisted mouth, if nothing blemished and imperfect may dwell there?"*
>
> *"It is true," said the Shepherd, "that you would have to be changed before you could live on the High Places, but if you are willing to go with me, I promise to help you develop hinds' feet. Up there on the mountains, as you get near the real High Places, the air is fresh and invigorating. It strengthens the whole body and there are streams with wonderful healing properties, so that those who bathe in them find all their blemishes and disfigurements washed away."*

The Shepherd also promised her a new name. It all sounded so wonderful. Did she have the faith to believe Him? She'd seen the evidence of His work in the lives of others. Friends she'd known who accepted His invitation and followed Him to the High Places were completely transformed. They lived very different lives now than what she lived—shut-up in the Fearing home like a prisoner, expected to wed her despicable cousin, Craven Fear.

One day, she couldn't bear her life living in shadow, waiting, any longer. She ran away to the foothills of the mountains and began to journey higher according to the directions given her by the Shepherd.

Imagine her disappointment upon learning that He will not accompany her directly, but instead, assigned two companions to assist her on the way: Sorrow and Suffering.

In my early years as a Christian, I read the story of *Hinds' Feet in High Places* on a yearly basis. It informed me, not only as a Christian, but as a writer. The power of story—of parable—to impart deeper truths to the understanding mind and transform lives has been foundational in my call to the written and spoken word. No wonder the landscapes of the Grand Tetons whisked me into this story-world, keeping me company on my real-life journey in high places.

Much-Afraid was, indeed, transformed on her way up the mountain. It was not an easy trek. But, for as much pain and loss suffered along the way, she received a double portion of riches with delight. She learned the way of the Kingdom of Love. Following in the way, she mastered the grace of obedience, one trusting leap of faith at a time.

Accepting the invitation, her Key of Faith unlocked the gateways to hinds' feet and heart's desires for Much-Afraid—renamed Grace and Glory. She began as a crippled apprentice, proved herself on the slopes as a journeyman, and achieved master status from the Master Himself at the zenith of the story when He says:

> *"So remember this; as long as you are willing to be Acceptance-with-Joy and Bearing-in-Love, you can never again become crippled, and you will be able to go wherever I lead you. You will be able to go down into the Valley of the world to work with me there, for that is where the evil and sorrowful and ugly things are which need to be overcome."*

Driving mountain roads, I saw my fair share of valleys dipping cavern-like below. Guardrails lined the asphalt roadway to protect motorists from accidently drifting too close to the sheer-drop cliff's edge rounding a corner.

Some boundaries are not to be crossed. Ever. We learn about the bounds of such borders when we study the map and stay alert to road-signs warning us along the way. Falling into the valley through a reckless breach of guardrails is not the same as traveling purposefully on a road leading to a valley. At the end of Much-Afraid's story, with her new name, Grace and Glory, the Chief Shepherd invites her to follow Him back to the valley from whence she came. She returns as a Gatekeeper in her own right, with invitations and keys for those called to hinds' feet in high places.

Like meditating on God's Word hidden in my heart, a good story absorbed into my being is a source of retreat to strengthen me when crossing thresholds and advancing forward, though the trials of life be cumbersome.

And soon, sure as the map promised, before nightfall the road through those cumbersome mountains ended. A late day sun split the clouds asunder and blue sky spread like the sea above me. Jagged peaks disappeared—left far behind. A great expanse of land rolled out and around, surrounding me like a plush carpet. We arrived in a new place with the promise of great adventure in a new home. True, I'd have to brave those Tetons again when we transferred back to the east coast in two years, but I knew better what to expect. I was stronger for conquering them. I'd be prepared on the next trip and could encourage others facing such a journey with what I'd learned through the wealth of this personal experience. A tiresome trial became great reward.

I was the much-changed Much-Afraid, relishing life in a new season with great delight, refreshed vision, and a new name—Grace and Glory.

Following a road map of directions set for us by another (submission to God or godly authority) is the choice that will make us the most free and able to grow into greater things. We may not think so at the time, but Gatekeepers, like the stubborn road map that gave me only one option for crossing the thresholds of the Grand Teton Mountains, do have my best interests at heart. They show me the way and equip me to cross over into my Field of Dreams—though the road be winding and weary.

I'm invited to go. You're invited to go. To follow the way. We can't see it all from beginning to end with our eyes. The map does not adjust its markings to our blindness. Much like the modern GPS system audibly telling us when to turn, where to turn, and how long to remain on any given road, if we trust its all-seeing satellite eye, we'll arrive at our destination. If we're willing to obey the directions.

~ The Gatekeeper's Key: Chapter 4—The Key of Faith ~

Otherwise, we'll hear the exasperation in a computerized voice saying, "Recalculating." Foolishly, by mistake or on purpose, sometimes we don't follow directions. Mercifully, every time, we get another chance to make it right. Thank God for Gatekeepers who see the end from the beginning and mentor us accordingly. They are worthy to follow.

It begins with the Key of Faith—the map opening wide the way. Follow through with a commitment to Trust and Obey—there is no other avenue for advancement. It requires diligence and discipline—especially when we're called to cross the barriers of mountain ranges in our lives. God is not concerned with the size of the thing that binds us in our way, so long as our way is His Way. The Key of Faith flattens obstacles like walls of Jericho tumbling down.

Breaking through the Grand Teton Mountains, though challenging, enriched me. In the end, I kept to the road. Did not fall asleep on the job. Did not run off the cliff. Controlled my temper when frustrated. Kept my cool when tempted by fear. In all, I conquered those mountains and took possession of the greater things on the other side of them that had been promised to me.

> *For you shall go out with joy,*
> *And be led out with peace;*
> *The mountains and the hills*
> *Shall break forth into singing before you,*
> *And all the trees of the field shall clap their hands.*
>   Isaiah 55:12 NKJV

Isaiah 55 is the Lord's invitation to follow Him in living an abundant life—whether that be spiritually, through a physical challenge, or the achievement of a life goal. When a Gatekeeper invites you to take the Key of Faith and go forth, he is inviting you to cross the threshold of a transformed life. God provides companions on the way to lead you forth, like those traveling with Much-Afraid. You may start the journey with Sorrow and Suffering but even they will be transformed along the way, renamed—Joy and Peace—just like in Much-Afraid's story.

The mountains and hills of obstacles, threatening to block your way to overcoming, break forth before you and into singing. God makes a way in your wilderness, moving mountains of doubt, fear, anxiety, stress, indecision . . . all the things, in fact, that kept Weaver wavering in the shadows on Waiting Lane. Obstacles turned to praise—often in unexpected ways.

The biblical imagery of Creation glorifying the Creator is a recurring theme in most of my writing. My season in Idaho Falls, living amid the generous treasuries of Creation, trained me to see the Lord in that which He has created. He is One with the strong trees of the field clapping me onto victory as I follow Him. Like the Shepherd invited Grace and Glory, so too, the Divine Coach invites me to unlock gates with His Key of Faith, Courage, and Love, crossing thresholds to where fields are white to harvest.

In application today, I'm following the Chief Shepherd forth in my calling as a writer, weaving words with power to transform lives of valley dwellers and mountain climbers. I produce my works and persevere through the mountains and hills of obstacles that rise-up before me. Daily I cry out to the Lord, petitioning Him in prayer, "Gimme a break!"

~ The Gatekeeper's Key: Chapter 4—The Key of Faith ~

And, by Faith, He does.

Doors unlock. Barriers break. In conquering them, my obstacles turn into opportunities for praise. In all this, I go forth with joyful delight. With a peace-filled heart. The breaks leading me forward prove fruitful as I trust in the Lord, choose to make the most of His provision, and not shrink back. This is what gives substance to things yet unseen; evidence to hopes—and Fields of Dreams.

> *Faith in the biblical sense is substantive, based on the knowledge that the One in whom that faith is placed has proven that He is worthy of that trust. In its essence, faith is a confidence in the person of Jesus Christ and in His power, so that even when His power does not serve my end, my confidence in Him remains because of who He is.*
>
> Ravi Zacharias

When God called the Israelites to cross over into the Promised Land, the Lord's promise of His Presence accompanied the call. He expected His people to take Him at His Word—by faith—believing as substance in complete confidence what they may not have been able to see with their physical eyes. A spiritual reality, nonetheless, making tangible the fulfillment of the promise in the material.

> *See, I am sending an angel before you to protect you on your journey and lead you safely to the place I have prepared for you.*
>
> Exodus 23:20 NLT

Climbing mountains and crossing over the obstacles they present to us in our lives is fraught with dangers, toils, and snares. They may be cumbersome weariness, boredom, and frustration at the monotony of the path, such as my scaling of the Grand Tetons; or more severe entanglements, like the adversaries Much-Afraid confronted on her journey to the High Places. Armies crossing borders into battle are at their most vulnerable. They rely on the leadership and authority of their General going with them, fearless facing the foe; a Gatekeeper inviting them into the fray of promised victory with shouts of joy, clapping their hands.

Like me, with my family, on the other side of the mountain, doing the happy dance when we finally arrived at our destination.

Journal and Discuss

What did Much-Afraid and Weaver have in common regarding how they perceived the Chief Shepherd and the Gatekeeper? What is the mountain in their lives they must overcome? Think about this while reading Psalm 34.

When you climb to the top of a mountain, the view is different than when standing at the foothills. Your vision grows larger from a mountaintop view, but many things block your sight from ground level. What is the vision for your life? What is God's vision for your life? Is your vision blocked by clouds or yet another mountain range? Or, do you try to see from the foothills? Explain the impact blocked vision has had in your life. How did you work through seasons of lost vision?

To take delight in the Lord, you draw close to Him and learn the desires of His heart. His desire becomes your desire. His vision becomes your vision. If true, how diligent do you think He is to give you the desires of your heart and fulfill your vision? What can you learn about crossing mountain ranges through Scripture:

> *Trust in the Lord, and do good;*
> *Dwell in the land, and feed on His faithfulness.*
> *Delight yourself also in the Lord,*
> *And He shall give you the desires of your heart.*
> *Commit your way to the Lord, trust also in Him,*
> *And He shall bring it to pass.*
> *He shall bring forth your righteousness as the light,*
> *And your justice as the noonday.*
>
> Psalm 37:3-6 NKJV

> *I focus on this one thing: Forgetting the past and looking forward to what lies ahead, I press on to reach the end of the race and receive the heavenly prize for which God, through Christ Jesus, is calling us.*
>
> Philippians 3:13-15 NLT

Define "delight" as the Appendix instructs. What would a response of delight look like regarding our attentions to the Lord? Was Weaver given to delight regarding the Gatekeeper? Why or why not? What kept her from receiving an invitation from the Gatekeeper? How can fear imprison delight and what is the outcome?

~ *The Gatekeeper's Key: Chapter 5—Gates and Glory* ~

Great doors swing on small hinges.

Dr. Lance Wallnau

Chapter 5: Gates and Glory
In Strength, Cross Thresholds

Lift up your heads, O you gates!
And be lifted up, you everlasting doors!
And the King of glory shall come in.
Who is this King of glory?
The LORD strong and mighty,
The LORD mighty in battle.
Psalm 24: 7-8 NKJV

I will build My church,
and the GATES of Hades shall not prevail against it.
Luke 16:18 NKJV

I will build my church,
and all the POWERS of hell will not conquer it.
Luke 16:18 NLT

GATE:
> In scripture, figuratively, power, dominion.
> *'Thy seed shall possess the gate of his enemies;'*
> *that is, towns and fortresses.* Genesis 22:17 KJV
> Webster's 1828 Dictionary

I am overwhelmed with grief at the seemingly impossible state of affairs manifesting in our nation and the world today. How far the founding landmarks of our Constitutional republic, built on biblical principles and rule of law, have moved! I've watched them be systematically replaced with evil counterfeits over my lifetime of close to six decades long. I see human hearts and minds sent strong delusions, believing lies, calling right wrong and wrong right, and a host of other travesties the Bible warns us about:

> *But know this, that in the last days perilous times will come: For men will be lovers of themselves, lovers of money, boasters, proud, blasphemers, disobedient to parents, unthankful, unholy, unloving, unforgiving, slanderers, without self-control, brutal, despisers of good, traitors, headstrong, haughty, lovers of pleasure rather than lovers of God, having a form of godliness but denying its power. And from such people turn away!*
>
> 2 Timothy 3:1-5 NKJV

All I know to do is to pray. But my prayer is reduced to a waterfall of tears. Words choke in my throat from sobbing. I feel helpless and alone facing the mountains of turmoil in current events, and wonder how to advance forward towards my life goals when the world seems on the tipping point to destruction. Panic grips me. The Field of Dreams I envision blurs and dissipates into nightmares. So, I cry out my complaint to the Lord:

> Who am I, Lord? What can I do?
>
> I am helpless to make a difference.
>
> I'm not strong enough to make an impact—
>
> just a tiny little mouse in this big scary scheme of things.
>
> It's all so dark and impossible.

I'm blubbering by this time.

Thankfully, our blubbering is not a bother to God. In fact, it is the passkey to open the door to His many mercies, and grace in our time of need.

> *Seeing then that we have a great High Priest who has passed through the heavens, Jesus the Son of God, let us hold fast our confession. For we do not have a High Priest who cannot sympathize with our weaknesses, but was in all points tempted as we are, yet without sin. Let us therefore come boldly to the throne of grace, that we may obtain mercy and find grace to help in time of need.*
>
> Hebrews 12:14-16 NKJV

"Yes," a commanding Voice whispers in my spirit. "You are a mouse. And you are many."

In that instant, I see a vision of . . . mice. Scurrying. On a mission. A beloved book opens in my imagination. My mind's eye flips to an image I know well: The Stone Table where the great Lion, Aslan, lay dead—sacrificed, shaved, and bound with ropes. His heart pierced and bleeding still.

C. S. Lewis does not spare the imagination of the reader in this climatic passage from *The Lion, the Witch, and the Wardrobe*. The Witch leaves him there to decay while she and all the powers of Hell believe themselves free to set out and thoroughly destroy all good things and beauty in the world of Narnia. In a lengthy discourse, Lewis describes the scene through the eyes of Susan and Lucy, the young children called to Narnia to lead in a time of war.

~ The Gatekeeper's Key: Chapter 5—Gates and Glory ~

Overwhelmed with grief at the impossible series of events they've witnessed, the young girls hide in the shadows after watching their King and Gatekeeper murdered before them. Their greatest hope is humiliated, undone at the hands of the Witch and her evil army. Carefully, when all is clear, they venture forth and remove the muzzle that clamps his mouth shut.

> *"I wonder could we untie him as well?" said Susan presently. But the enemies, out of pure spitefulness had drawn the cords so tight that the girls could make nothing of the knots.*

They had not the strength to untie the binding cords. Yet, as they kiss his lifeless face, weeping and blubbering in uncontained sorrow, Lucy notices small movements upon his dead body.

A mouse. First one . . . then another . . . and another. A legion of them suddenly materialize on the scene. Susan responds, wildly waving her arms to shoo them away. But Lucy sees something more.

> *"Wait!" said Lucy who had been looking at them more closely still. "Can you see what they're doing . . . I think they're friendly mice. Poor little things—they don't realize he's dead. They think it'll do some good untying him." They could see the mice nibbling away; dozens and dozens, even hundreds, of little field mice. And at last, one by one, the ropes were all gnawed through . . . The girls cleared away the remains of the gnawed ropes. Aslan looked more like himself without them. Every moment his dead face*

looked nobler, as the light grew and they could see it better.

A mouse nibbled away at the ropes keeping Aslan tied down to the Stone Table. Susan and Lucy thought it a nice gesture, but a waste of time and effort.

Many say the same about prayer.

The girls stroll a short distance away to move about, in order to warm themselves. They wonder, grief-stricken, at what they have seen. But a loud clap, "a great cracking, deafening noise," sends them running back to where they left Aslan in the murky darkness before the dawn.

> *The rising of the sun had made everything look so different—all the colours and shadows were changed—that for a moment they didn't see the important thing. Then they did. The Stone Table was broken into two pieces by a great crack that ran down it from end to end; and there was no Aslan . . . "Who's done it?" cried Susan. "What does it mean? Is it more magic?"*
>
> *"Yes!" said a great voice behind their backs. "It is more magic." They looked round. There, shining in the sunrise larger than they had seen him before, shaking his mane (for it had apparently grown again) stood Aslan himself . . .*

Because . . .

> *". . . when a willing victim who had committed no treachery was killed in a traitor's stead, the Table*

> *would crack and Death itself would start working backwards." . . . Aslan stood up and when he opened his mouth to roar his face became so terrible that they did not dare to look at it. And they saw all the trees in front of him bend before the blast of his roaring as grass bends in a meadow before the wind. Then he said, "We have a long journey to go. You must ride on me."*

In his 1858 book, *Songs and Ballads*, Samuel Lover, recounts the poetic and musical traditions of the Irish:

> *There is a beautiful saying amongst the Irish peasantry to inspire hope under adverse circumstances: "Remember," they say, "that the darkest hour of all, is the hour before day."*

He may have borrowed from words penned by Thomas Fuller, English historian and theologian in his 1650 travelogue of Palestine remarking, "It is always darkest just before the Day dawneth." This is the earliest record of this familiar cliché meant to give hope in the most dire of circumstances. In fact, it is true that the progression of time—day to night and night to day—is a certainty. Just when you think it can't get any darker—it does. And in the next second after the very darkest of seconds, there is a crack of light to herald the approaching day.

Lucy and Susan thought the sacrificial death of Aslan was the darkest dark. They wondered, *Who would lead the battle now?* Adding insult to injury, all those tiny mice swarming his body as in a feeding frenzy, nibbling away at the ropes, made everything so final and darker still. Even so:

~ The Gatekeeper's Key: Chapter 5—Gates and Glory ~

Bonds broke in the dark of night.
Aslan rose by the dawn's early light.

The efforts of ones with little strength, doing what they knew to do by faith, played a key part to greater purposes. The everlasting gates swung wide and the Lion rose alive.

This is the Resurrection power in Jesus Christ—to make darkness light and death be life. The salvation of believers is wrought up in this, the crux of the Christian faith. And this saving faith can be applied to dark dilemmas that confront us on every battlefield we face, standing before locked gates of overwhelming power.

Lift up your heads, O you gates!
And be lifted up, you everlasting doors!
And the King of glory shall come in.
Who is this King of glory?
The LORD *strong and mighty,*
The LORD *mighty in battle.*

Psalm 24: 7-8 NKJV

I will build My church,
and the GATES of Hades shall not prevail against it.

Luke 16:18 NKJV

We prayerfully petition the Gatekeeper with the key to open the gates of powers that constrain us. Like mice, diligent to nibble away at Aslan's ropes, our prayers in faith, break the fibers of binding impossibilities. The way of possibility stretches wide open before us. We pass freely into new territories, new chapters in the story, and plot twists we may never have imagined.

~ The Gatekeeper's Key: Chapter 5—Gates and Glory ~

Lucy and Susan's story does not end in this scene of a happy reunion with their beloved Aslan. There is yet a war raging for the freedom of a country long held captive. Holding fast to him, they race to the frontlines of the battle, storming powerful gates of evil to glory, mounted upon the strength of he who:

> *. . . doesn't need to be guided and never grows tired. He rushes on and on, never missing his footing, never hesitating, threading his way with perfect skill between tree-trunks, jumping over bush and briar and the smaller streams, wading the larger, swimming the largest of all . . . the Lion had gathered himself together for a greater leap than any he had yet made and jumped—or you may call it flying rather than jumping—right over the castle wall. The two girls were breathless, but unhurt . . .*

Breathless. Yes—that's how I feel of late in what seems a world gone mad. I am out of breath. I also am aware that I've been sighing deep sighs intermittently throughout the day. I feel the assaults in the spiritual realm and see the turmoil in the physical realm. I need to catch my breath. So, I pray—little as I am. Nibble. Nibble. Nibble.

Unhurt. Mounted on the back of my Lord Jesus, I arrive to meet the demands of the day—whatever they may be—unhurt. A little worse for wear, perhaps, as we all bear the burdens of calamitous times. But my fate is sealed in His Spirit, by His blood and the word of my testimony.

> *Now salvation, and strength, and the kingdom of our God, and the power of His Christ have come, for the*

> *accuser of our brethren, who accused them before our God day and night, has been cast down. And they overcame him by the blood of the Lamb and by the word of their testimony . . .*
>
> Revelations 12:10-11 NKJV

I am a mouse and I'm not alone. You may be a mouse, too. Our prayers are our strength, powerful to nibble away at the cords that appear to bind my Lord and Ultimate Gatekeeper, as He bides His time for the dawn of due season to rise-up and roar. My mouse-like prayers, taken together with your mouse-like prayers, petition the Lord to let loose the Lion of Judah and exercise His might in our fight.

Small. Strong. Significant.

We have such need of the Lord to lead in the battle for our daily bread, our Field of Dreams, deliverance from evil, the hearts and minds of this present generation, and the soul of our nation.

Because, you see, THAT is the threshold He invites us to cross, through a gateway of history—His Story—in the chapter of current events through which we now live. It's God's continuing story of His relationship with mankind and the unfolding of His purposes in the earth. He invites us to play our part on a Field of Dreams unique to each of us, and on many fronts. Like tiny mice standing before massive thick tower walls, our way is often blocked.

But for the Lion Who goes before us.

Perhaps, in fleshing out this scene, C. S. Lewis gave a nod to the ancient storyteller, Aesop, whose fable of *The Lion and the Mouse* is still a childhood favorite. But do we take such a treasure from our nursery room into the halls of our grown-up world?

In Aesop's tale, the little mouse, caught by the lion, petitioned him to be set free, offering to one day return the favor. The bold promise from one so small entertained the King of the Beasts. For being a source of laughter that day, the lion released the mouse to live. Sometime later, the lion found himself caught up in the nets of a trap set by hunters. The mouse happened upon him and nibbled away at the ropes, setting the lion free to live, so keeping the promise once made to him. Their lives preserved and relationship sealed by a shared promise.

Our strength in passing through gates to glory is not bound up in ourselves alone—but in our partnership with He Who invites us to cross borders of the impossible with Him to fulfill a shared vision.

I may tremble at the thought of taking the risks necessary to write, speak, and publish my work—like Weaver—but once invited to go forth with the key to unlock gates, I do so not in my own stature, but in the strength of the Lord, my Gatekeeper. I am small. He is great. I acknowledge this truth and my dependence upon Him with every prayer I nibble out each day along the way.

I am a great sinner, but Christ is a greater Saviour.

John Newton

~ The Gatekeeper's Key: Chapter 5—Gates and Glory ~

I dread my social media newsfeed. I hate the headlines. I do tend to shrink back into the shadows on Waiting Lane, thinking myself too small—like a mouse—to venture into the courtyard of the Gatekeepers in my life and the world at large. But, the Gatekeeper's invitation calls me there. This compels me to nibble away the day in prayer without ceasing, I accomplish my mouse-like mission in the power of a Lion. I know not how long I must gnaw at the ropes, wrestling in prayer, before the bonds break and the Lion roars. But to be true to my mission in concert with many others—mice like me—I can be confident that I'm in the center of God's will for my life.

Aslan was dead. *"Poor little things—they don't realize he's dead. They think it'll do some good untying him."* Lucy thought the mice and their efforts foolish towards an impossible hope.

In the face of impossible personal goals, and national and global unrest as never before seen in history, God's grace and mercy stands at the door of unknown outcomes. For me, I choose boldness—standing before His Throne, the Gatekeeper—in petition. I'll live in expectation of the impossible and keep nibbling away.

Jesus has the last roar.

I highly recommend the prolific works of C. S. Lewis. His books are classics, revealing biblical truths with powerful reasoning and lucid explanations, both directly in his non-fiction writings, and metaphorically in his fiction, specifically *The Chronicles of Narnia* series.

The Lion, the Witch, and the Wardrobe, where we first meet Aslan as a type of Christ, paints a dynamic picture of the plan of salvation and elements of the spiritual battle taking place behind the scenes.

There is always a spiritual battle taking place behind the scenes—especially when Gatekeepers invite us to possess the key, to unlock gates, to overcome borders in our lives that must be crossed so we may walk in the calling and opportunities that are our destiny in Christ.

Journal and Discuss

How does seeing yourself as a mouse nibbling away at binding circumstances through prayer give you hope that the roar of the Lion of Judah may be released to work His will and wonders in your dark and difficult times?

The length of the hinge on the front door to my house is four inches. The door is six times the length of the three hinges necessary to swing it wide, opening to a new day, or shutting it secure against invaders in the night. The hinges are small but vital partners working together with the tiny key turning the lock. What happens when the hinge of a door becomes stuck? The Gatekeeper may give you the key—the strength to unlock the door—but what must happen to the hinges for the door to open? How does persevering in prayer oil your efforts to penetrate gates to glory?

In Weaver's story, she often lingered on the outskirts of the courtyard filled with others actively petitioning the Gatekeeper for an invitation and a key. Even so, the Gatekeeper knew she was there. He was watching her—like a shepherd looking after the shy sheep fearful to draw too close to him near the gate. At the shepherd's gate, the sheep knew to draw near, boldly seeking him for the blessings he would pour upon them: food, water, healing of wounds, comfort. Only then could they be empowered to grow in strength and accomplish their purpose. Read the following passage of Scripture, think on these things as they may relate to you. A mouse. A hinge. A sheep. Write a prayer of petition and praise based upon your conclusions.

> *I tell you the truth, anyone who sneaks over the wall of a sheepfold, rather than going through the gate, must surely be a thief and a robber! But the one who enters through the gate is the shepherd of the sheep. The gatekeeper opens the gate for him, and the sheep recognize his voice and come to him. He calls his own sheep by name and leads them out.*
>
> John 10:1-3 NLT

Meet Him at the gate and he will pour out his blessings upon you.

Ray Carman
EnjoytheShepherd.com

~ The Gatekeeper's Key: Chapter 6—Portals to Potential ~

When a plunge is to be made in the water,
it is of no use lingering on the bank.

Charles Dickens

Chapter 6: Portals to Potential
In Opportunity, Go Forth

See then that you walk circumspectly, not as fools but as wise, redeeming the time, because the days are evil. Therefore, do not be unwise, but understand what the will of the Lord is.

Ephesians 5:15-17 NKJV

There are many kinds of Gatekeepers in the world, the masters who guard the doorposts of opportunity. They are the employers interviewing you for a job. Or teachers in a classroom inviting you to open your book to the next chapter and read the lesson. Mentors recognize your gifts and call you to destiny. They come alongside you to escort you through portals to your potential via relationships built within shared circumstances.

Sometimes they are soldiers keeping watch, so no unworthy individual crosses the threshold of a gateway to valuable things, physical places like a castle, home, bank, village, city, country borders, locked rooms with treasures, and the like. But, sometimes, Gatekeepers block the entrance to intangibles, like opportunity, freedom, healing, love, provision, power, knowledge, understanding, skill, desire, and wisdom.

They can be heroes or enemies.

Gatekeepers know to whom they may allow an invitation for the privilege of stepping into the next level of a desired object. All those who would pass must prove their worth. It may be a token in the slot that one has paid the fare, or paper credentials verifying one's title, a diploma, or deed of ownership. Perhaps it is a random test to examine the heart or skill-set of an individual to assess readiness for passage through the gate, or promotion to the next grade level in school, or job position.

As a writer and artist, I honed my craft over the years seeking Gatekeepers at every turn. Teachers. Mentors. These are those who have gone before me, who have learned the way of maturity, and can nurture me to the next level of my strength and calling. These are the peer professionals who can open doors to provision, to jobs, to the next amazing thing I might write that has the power to transform a life.

They are people I've been in relationship with for decades of my life, or mere days only, leaving a deposit of direction, and then, never to connect again.

The mark these masters make on my life transforms me inside and out. I want to follow in their footsteps as the young page to *Good King Wenceslas*, invited by his lord to learn the way of Christian benevolence. I love these key verses of the 1853 poem detailing the journey to bring food and firewood to a poor peasant man in winter:

> *"Sire, the night is darker now*
> *And the wind blows stronger*
> *Fails my heart, I know not how,*
> *I can go no longer."*

"Mark my footsteps, my good page
Tread thou in them boldly
Thou shalt find the winter's rage
Freeze thy blood less coldly."

In his master's steps he trod
Where the snow lay dinted
Heat was in the very sod
Which the Saint had printed

John Mason Neale

But, not all Gatekeepers are saints. Some appear to be enemies at first, like the ministrations of Sorrow and Suffering to Much-Afraid. Or the stern disciplines of Brother Luke to work bitterness from young Robin's heart.

Many will be sinners who misuse and abuse you along the way. Such was the case when Christian and his companion, Hopeful, wandered where they ought not, and fell into the hands of the cruel Giant Despair. On every occasion, the Giant falsely accused them. And beat them. And left them to rot in his dungeon at Doubting Castle.

> *Then he attacked them and beat them fearfully in such a way that they were not able to help themselves or to turn themselves over on the floor. This done, he withdrew and left them there to sympathize with their misery and to mourn under their distress.*

I quote here from the classic by John Bunyan, *Pilgrim's Progress*, a story delivered to him in a dream over a period of time while languishing in prison for his faith. It is a powerful allegory of the Christian walk—another "journey" story like the 20th century, *Hinds' Feet in High Places*, but written almost 400 years earlier.

Imprisoned as they were, their Gatekeeper, a vile monster of a giant, oppressed them on every occasion in an effort to drive them to complete desolation. Christian came close to taking the Key of Despair.

> *"Brother," said Christian, "what shall we do? The life we're now living is miserable! As for me, I don't know whether it's best to live like this or to die quickly . . . and the grave seems more easy for me than this dungeon! Shall we be ruled by the Giant?"*

Hopeful pointed out the negative eternal consequences of giving into Giant Despair, killing both body and soul, were they to kill themselves to escape their circumstances.

> *[Said Hopeful,] ". . . I'm resolved to muster up a manly heart and to try my best to get out from under his hand. I was a fool that I didn't try to do it before. But, let's be patient, Brother, and endure awhile longer. The time may come that provides us a happy release, but let's not be our own murders."*

Bless his heart—Hopeful was certainly the fellow to have by your side in dire conditions. They endured, with many more "hopeful" sermons by Hopeful to bolster Christian as they suffered together. Day after day the Giant tortured them, seeking for them to choose to give up on their own rather than for him to kill them outright.

Until . . .

> *Well, on Saturday about midnight, the prisoners began to pray, and they continued in prayer until almost daybreak. A little before dawn good Christian, as someone half amazed, broke out in this passionate declaration: "What a fool I am," he exclaimed, "to lay here in a stinking dungeon, when I could just as easily walk at liberty! In my coat, next to my heart, I have a Key called Promise. I'm persuaded it will open any lock in Doubting Castle."*

To be sure, the key unlocked every door in the castle and opened wide a way of escape, restoring Christian and Hopeful to the right path from which they had strayed. They were wounded, but healed. And scarred—much like the risen Jesus still bears His scars. But, they were alive and on their way. Delayed, but not despairing.

Only in hindsight do we honor Gatekeepers in our lives like Giant Despair. In the crucible of his dungeons, we learn thanksgiving for the gates hardship unlocks and the opportunities our contention with unsavory circumstances open for us.

In Pilgrim's case, his trial in Doubting Castle made it possible for him to leave a signpost to warn other pilgrims on the same journey. Through the footstep of a mentor, he turned his trial into a blessing for others. This reminds us of Jesus, Who took the punishment of sin on the cross Himself, showing us the way as a signpost of salvation. He bore the pain so we don't have to. He is the Key of Promise unlocking the gates (the power) of Giant Despair and Doubting Castle to set us free of our sin and restore us to life.

The Key of Promise is vital to crossing through the Portals of Potential.

We learn to find gain in our losses and to be fortified in battle, steeled stronger for our future. There is a fine line between victim and victory. The wise weaver will not nurse her wounds long, dare she wallow in the mire, stuck in a moment, lose heart in despair, and remove herself back to Wannabe Village Center where:

> *They keep to their comfort zones at the center, giving little thought to worlds outside, knowing only of what they see in the scope of their narrowed vision.*

Harboring bitterness for the trials of the journey will never allow your ship to cross the waters into deeper seas of opportunity. You won't grow into greater things tied to the dock, lingering on the bank. A plunge is necessary.

> Disturb us Lord,
>
> to dare more boldly,
>
> to venture on wilder seas,
>
> where storms show your mastery;
>
> where in losing sight of land,
>
> we shall find the stars.
>
> — Sir Francis Drake

Ultimately, God is the Gatekeeper of our lives, who sets Gatekeepers before us, be they through smooth or stormy oceans of opportunity.

OPPORTUNITY:
> Fit or convenient time; a time favorable for the purpose; suitable time combined with other favorable circumstances. A wise man will make more opportunities than he finds.
> *Noah Webster's 1828 Dictionary*

Invitations are forthcoming should we be bold enough to seek them out and recognize the convenient time and circumstances to step forward and face them. We answer the call to move from the center of Wannabe Village to the margins of ministry on Waiting Lane, the place of preparation. We must learn discernment as we linger there and pursue with diligence He who is our delight. Confidently, we prove our passion, produce within our craft, and persevere in the marketplace.

For Weaver, fear of failure stifled delight in her desire. But so too, fear of success frequently paralyzes. Failure might keep her shrinking back from actively petitioning the Gatekeeper; and success is a formidable prize, often feared.

But, if you have received an invitation you have been called. If you possess the Key of Promise, you are armed to boldly walk out of Doubting Castle. Sallie forth into the courtyard of opportunity and seize the day, redeeming the time and God's provisions for you.

Weaver didn't expect opportunity to drop into her lap, packaged as a toss away invitation belonging to another. When forced to face the fearsome spectre of her dreams actually coming to fruition, the temptation to shrink back is very real. But for the desire—the delight—of her heart.

Will she go, seize the day, redeem the time, and possess the land before her?

What would you do with such an invitation and only one word to be going on with—especially if it came from an unexpected source? An unexpected stroke, like the fencing term, cuts down an enemy with a sword thrust to reveal a champion. Nineteenth century author and poet, Edward Sill, expresses this well in his classic poem titled, *Opportunity*:

> *This I beheld, or dreamed it in a dream—*
> *There spread a cloud of dust along a plain;*
> *And underneath the cloud, or in it, raged*
> *A furious battle, and men yelled, and swords*
> *Shocked upon swords and shields.*
> *A prince's banner*
> *Wavered, then staggered backward,*
> *Hemmed by foes.*
> *A craven hung along the battle's edge,*
> *And thought, "Had I a sword of keener steel—*
> *That blue blade that the king's son bears—but this*
> *Blunt thing—!"*
> *He snapped and flung it from his hand,*
> *And lowering crept away and left the field.*
> *Then came the king's son, wounded sore bested,*
> *And weaponless, and saw the broken sword*
> *Hilt-buried in the dry and trodden sand,*
> *And ran and snatched it, and with battle-shout*
> *Lifted afresh he hewed his enemy down*
> *And saved a great cause that heroic day.*

It is a daunting invitation. But, when I am invited to GO, by the Gatekeeper of my life, I am invited to seize the opportunities and provisions in God's house. He invites me to pass through the gate, crossing the threshold of my portal to potential—the field of my hopes and dreams. And, God's will for my life.

> *Dragging my feet*
> *Kicking and complaining,*
> *Stumbling through the dark*
> *To the brink of obedience.*
> *I plunge forward*
> *Where the door opens to me*
> *A portal to the impossible*
> *Is all light and possibility.*
> *Crossing the threshold, I arrive*
> *Able, equipped, comprehending.*
> *I can do all things good and beauty*
> *Through Christ*
> *Who strengthens me.*
>
> Kathryn Ross
(Inspired by Philippians 4:13)

Journal and Discuss

The Bible is filled with examples of gates, gatekeepers, promised lands, and keys to possessing the promise of abundant life. Some were discussed in the previous chapters. Volumes more could be written exploring the nuances of each example in God's Word.

Do your own Bible study from the list below and record what you learn from these stories about gates, promised lands, and keys. Chart the similarities that you find for each:
- ❖ The lamb's blood on the doorposts at Passover
- ❖ The crossing of the Red Sea
- ❖ The borders of the Promised Land
- ❖ The walls of Jericho
- ❖ The construction of the Temple
- ❖ Nehemiah rebuilding Jerusalem's walls and gates
- ❖ How many more can you find?

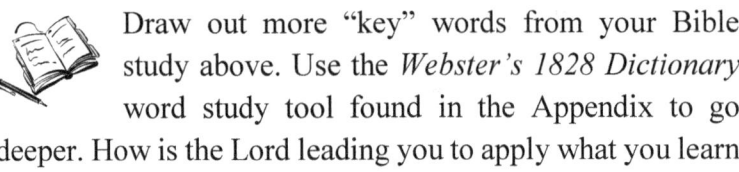 Draw out more "key" words from your Bible study above. Use the *Webster's 1828 Dictionary* word study tool found in the Appendix to go deeper. How is the Lord leading you to apply what you learn to your life?

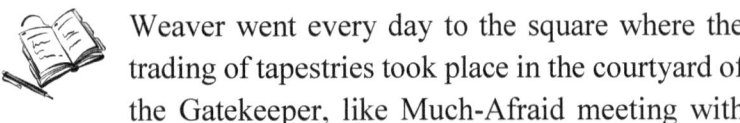 Weaver went every day to the square where the trading of tapestries took place in the courtyard of the Gatekeeper, like Much-Afraid meeting with the Chief Shepherd by the pool in the Valley. Both were places of opportunity. Weaver greatly desired to be invited to own a Gatekeeper's Key. Why was an invitation not forthcoming to her even though she brought her tapestry to the square? What is the gate between you and your Field of Dreams? What opportunity can breach the gate?

 Imagine the scene painted of the battlefield in the poem *Opportunity*. What similarities are there to Weaver's story or as related to biblical themes? For instance, did Israel expect their Messiah to be born as a babe in a stable? Did they ever imagine He would have to

die to secure salvation? Like a broken sword tossed carelessly away by one looking for something more, in the hand of another desperate for life, the sword of Jesus on the cross hews down the enemy and truly "saved a great cause that heroic day." Write your thoughts on these things and then compose a poem as an illustration of your meditations.

~ The Gatekeeper's Key: Chapter 7—One Way Through ~

I tell you the truth, I am the gate ... Those who come in through me will be saved. They will come and go freely and will find good pastures.

John 10:7,9 NLT

Chapter 7: One Way Through
Jesus—The Ultimate Gatekeeper

*"I tell you the truth, anyone who sneaks over the wall of a
sheepfold, rather than going through the gate,
must surely be a thief and a robber!
But the one who enters through the gate
is the shepherd of the sheep.
The gatekeeper opens the gate for him, and the sheep
recognize his voice and come to him.
He calls his own sheep by name and leads them out.
After he has gathered his own flock,
he walks ahead of them, and they follow him
because they know his voice.
They won't follow a stranger;
they will run from him because they don't know his voice."
Those who heard Jesus use this illustration didn't
understand what he meant, so he explained it to them:
"I tell you the truth, I am the gate for the sheep.
All who came before me were thieves and robbers.
But the true sheep did not listen to them.
Yes, I am the gate.
Those who come in through me will be saved.
They will come and go freely and will find good pastures.
The thief's purpose is to steal and kill and destroy.
My purpose is to give them a rich and satisfying life.*
John 10:1-10 NLT

*We must quickly carry out the tasks assigned us by the one
who sent us.*
John 9:4 NLT

Sight is a precious gift. As I've aged, my eyesight requires the oversight of an optician, and periodic upticks in prescription glasses. I reach for them the first thing in the morning when I awake. Should I venture from my bedroom into the hallway and kitchen without them, I struggle with a sense of loss. Something is missing. I am apt to stumble. Though I can see fairly well enough to find my way, I feel my lack and am disoriented unless my glasses are firmly in place, correcting my vision with precision.

Our life is like that when we try to attempt living without a clear vision of where we're going. We stumble along, or worse, freeze in place, fearful to move forward. We shrink back, like Weaver prior to the day she met the Story-Master Gatekeeper face to face. Her life would never be the same after the challenging encounter. How was her vision corrected? Did she "go" after all?

A speaker at a conference I recently attended thoroughly captivated my imagination when she opened her session with an interesting fact about the impala, a gazelle-like animal found in the wilds of African safari lands.

"The impala," she said, "can jump ten feet in the air and thirty feet out." The room hushed, waiting to learn the significance of such a statement. She repeated it again for emphasis. Then, after a dramatic pause she posited this probing question: "How do you keep an impala in a zoo?"

Silence followed as we pondered an intelligent answer. A few brave ladies offered suggestions. Our speaker raised her chin, knowingly, and smiled. "The impala," she said, weighting each word deliberately, "will not jump if it cannot see where it is going to land. A zookeeper only needs a wall high enough that the animal cannot see over it, to keep the creature in containment.

I was undone!

What a powerful illustration of faith—or the lack thereof. Once again, much like Dorothy who always had the power to go home with the click or her heels, the impala need only leap up to look out, allowing his vision to expand, and, with such enlightened sight, further leap to freedom. I think of my dream and the ease of peeling back the chicken wire that fenced me in, opening a portal through which to cross the threshold of potential. I was blind to it, at first.

Jesus often spoke of short-sightedness and the lack of faith due to lack of vision. He healed many blind men—never using the same method twice. In each instance, He met the blindness head-on in a unique manner.

> *As Jesus was walking along, he saw a man who had been blind from birth. "Rabbi," his disciples asked him, "why was this man born blind? Was it because of his own sins or his parents' sins?"*
> *"It was not because of his sins or his parents' sins," Jesus answered. "This happened so the power of God could be seen in him. We must quickly carry out the tasks assigned us by the one who sent us. The night is coming, and then no one can work. But while I am here in the world, I am the light of the world."*
> *Then he spit on the ground, made mud with the saliva, and spread the mud over the blind man's eyes. He told him, "Go wash yourself in the pool of Siloam" (Siloam means "sent"). So the man went and washed and came back seeing!*
> John 9:1-7 NLT

Jesus uses the blindness of a man to illustrate truths:

1. **Jesus Allows** for life in a "blind season" because it has purpose for God to glorify Himself in ways we cannot imagine, that the "power of God could be seen in Him." Our seasons of blindness drive us to a place of desperation and dependence upon God, which manifests a greater glory, not our own.

2. **Jesus Invites** the blind man to participate in his own healing by washing in the Pool of Siloam (meaning "sent"). Only by stepping out into the waters of faith, taking the risk to believe though he could not see, would the blind man become a new man of vision. We, too, are invited to participate in healing works in our unique callings—sent by the Sent One.

3. **Jesus Exhorts** his followers with urgency to work in their "tasks assigned," in their calling, and to do so in His Light. Dark times would come when there would be no Light in which to see, but in His Light there is sight and the work of our calling is assured.

Jesus is the Ultimate Gatekeeper through Whom we pass to enter into new life, sight, and service within our calling. Whether it is the call to the work of a weaver of words, or the keeper of the home, or the leader of communities or the influencer of minds, there is one gate only through which we must pass to cross the threshold of God's full potential for our lives. This portal is Christ Himself—the Good Shepherd. Hearing His Voice and following His Lead into the Field of our Dreams—the call on our lives—is His perfect Will for us. He called us and will do it.

That blind man, who received his sight, did so because he obeyed the Lord and walked out his faith as the Lord called him to do—in due season. The biblical account continues, detailing the man's ordeal in convincing the people and religious leaders that he was, indeed, healed by the Word of Jesus. Such a miracle was beyond belief by everyone except the blind man who could now see. Poor fellow—he was mocked and called a liar. But, no matter. He. Could. See!

> *"We know that God doesn't listen to sinners, but he is ready to hear those who worship him and do his will. Ever since the world began, no one has been able to open the eyes of someone born blind. If this man were not from God, he couldn't have done it."*
>
> John 9:31-33 NLT

I imagine this beggar with new eyes was not too put off when put out of the synagogue for speaking his mind so thoroughly. He was dangerous now, his very life a testimony to the power and truth of Jesus Christ. The religious leaders, born with the ability to see, showed themselves more blind than he had been his whole life. Jesus redeemed his blind season, making it, in hindsight, something to be thankful for in the end. A new abundance, greatly cherished, his fortunes turned. Sight stirred insight. No longer a caged impala, now he could leap up and out, taking joy as he passed through the Gate into God's promises on the other side of his calling.

There's an old Latin phrase that reads, "Ad astra per aspera," meaning "To the stars through difficulties."

Are you in a blind season where you know you're stuck? Do you fear the risk of leaping up and out through the gate into the fullness of God's promised abundance and calling for your life? Know this: The difficulties that keep you stumbling in the dark are not what confines you. They are the very thing upon which to build your testimony of God's faithfulness through the dark and difficult, to the heights of a sky lit by starlight, sparkling like heavenly jewels from the coffers of Christ in your life.

Reach for those stars. They are your Field of Dreams. Jesus stands at the Gate and beckons you to enter through Him, and so realize His plans and purposes for your life. Listen for His voice. He leads and guides you each step of the way. He is the Gatekeeper. His Invitation has been delivered to you through His Calling—the Key is His Cross.

Will you GO?

Journal and Discuss

Jesus, the Ultimate Gatekeeper, calls all believers to seize the day of opportunity:

> *And Jesus came and spoke to them, saying, "All authority has been given to Me in heaven and on earth. Go therefore and make disciples of all the nations, baptizing them in the name of the Father and of the Son and of the Holy Spirit, teaching them to observe all things that I have commanded you; and lo, I am with you always, even to the end of the age.*
> Matthew 28:18-20 NKJV

Doors of opportunity are opening in every field of influence in the earth beyond the church doors: government, business, academics, entertainment, and media. These are fields white to harvest, suffering from a lack of salt—the God flavors Christians provide. How can you affirm your Purpose, develop your Product, and Persevere in answering your unique call to cross the thresholds of the Great Commission?

Are there Fields of Dreams you seek to embrace this year? Are you waiting for an invitation and the Key of Opportunity to unlock the potential you envision? Petition the Gatekeeper of your life. He seeks those whose hearts are turned towards Him as their desire. Journal concluding thoughts as prayer on the following page.

Benediction

Now may the God of peace

make you holy in every way,

and may your whole spirit

and soul and body be kept blameless

until our Lord Jesus Christ comes again.

God will make this happen,

for he who calls you is faithful.

1 Thessalonians 5:23-24 NLT

~ The Gatekeeper's Key: Chapter 7—One Way Through ~

My Gatekeeper's Key Prayer

~ The Gatekeeper's Key: Chapter 7—One Way Through ~

~ The Gatekeeper's Key: Appendix—Defining Terms ~

Language, as well as the faculty of speech, was the immediate gift of God.

Noah Webster

Appendix

Defining the Terms Word Study

*Let the words of my mouth and the meditation of my heart,
be acceptable in Your sight,
O Lord, my strength and my Redeemer.*
                                        Psalm 19:14 NKJV

My mom grew up on a chicken farm in the country. Because of living so far from town, she was not able to participate in extra-curricular activities. Her transportation to and from school depended upon a school bus and a one-mile trek to the bus stop—there and back again. She spent her youth with much time on her hands.

Once she finished her chores and homework, she snuggled into a corner in the room she shared with her sister, my aunt, where the two enjoyed many hours buried in the glories of a good book. Mother preferred stories and poetry, while my aunt eagerly ruminated over the pages of the dictionary as pleasure reading. To this day, my aunt is a voracious reader and lover of words, using them well.

My memories growing up involved books and Mother modeling the joy of reading. She encouraged me in my writing from when I first began to possess words and the power to wield them—read, written, and spoken. When I didn't know the meaning of a word, or used it incorrectly Mother's response was always the same. "Look it up."

So, I did.

For years, I sought out the *Webster's Dictionary* to aid my spelling and word use. But it was not until my own children were in school, and I trained in Principle Approach Education®, that I learned about the Webster behind the dictionary and the foundational work bearing his name, *Noah Webster's 1828 American Dictionary of the English Language.*

A Slice of American History

The Providential history of our nation fascinates the intellect as it inspires the spirit to note God's hand in the birth of a country like none other in all human history. Noah Webster lived through the raucous years of revolution, turned to independence, and the drafting of the Constitution of the United States—a governmental framework founded on Judeo-Christian values and the precepts of biblical principles. This was unique in world history.

The language used in the writings of our founding generations and government documents were both precise and elevated, drafted for an educated and moral society. It was imperative that American citizens properly define terms in the manner used and understood at the time. Noah Webster devoted twenty years of his life to the meticulous research of each word as used within our distinctly unique American culture. To define words, he studied the biblical use of each found in the Scriptures, as well as the accepted use in classical literature, drawn from their roots in European, Latin, Greek, and Hebrew language and cultures.

It was a mountain of work, fired by his passion to leave a primary source legacy of language and education tools for subsequent generations of Americans. In doing so, all citizens could be equipped to properly steward the gift of liberty in a distinctly Christian nation. Along with the Bible, his *Blue Back Speller* formed the foundation of American classroom teaching for years. The speller approached the teaching and learning of words and meanings using readings from the Bible, classics, and essays in Christian living.

Principle Approach Education® restored these hallmarks of an American Christian education to our culture in the 20th century after many decades of decline, through the work of Rosalie J. Slater and Verna Hall, beginning in the 1940s. At the center of their documentation and re-publication of the primary sources detailing our nation's American Christian history and founding, is their re-publication of the original *1828 Dictionary* by Webster in facsimile form. Currently, it is available as a searchable tool with just the click of your computer's mouse online at websterdictionary1828.com.

I never study a subject without it!

To that end, in this chapter I have excerpted key words and their pertinent definitions from the *1828 Dictionary*, which you will find useful in reading through this book. Words mean things and words painstakingly defined through the historical lens of biblical truth raise our understanding of both the word and how it is used.

Modern dictionaries scrub the eloquence and depth of Webster's original 1828 definitions, redefining them to suit changes in society. But, I much prefer his gourmet menu, swinging wide the gates of understanding, to today's junk food that strips language of its glory and power to persuade on the merit and meat of meaning.

I invite you to read through this selection of key words and use the online *1828 Dictionary* tool to expand your study of words and meanings in your journal exercises. Even when you know what the word means in context, you must dive deeper into that word to mine its true riches.

Slow down. Don't rush. Ponder all these things in your heart. Prepare your palate to taste nuances in comprehension that you might have missed were you to speed-read rather than deep read. The stories, discussion questions, and journal prompts in each chapter of this book will move you to reference the meanings of these key words again and again.

Refer to tips for personal word studies using Principle Approach methods at the end of this chapter. For more information about Principle Approach Education® and *Noah Webster's 1828 Dictionary*, refer to the NOTES at the end of this book. Bon Appetit!

GATE:
1. A large door which gives entrance into a walled city, a castle, a temple, palace or other large edifice . . . gate signifies both the opening or passage, and the frame of boards, planks or timber which closes the passage.
2. An avenue; an opening; a way.
3. In scripture, figuratively, power, dominion. *'Thy seed shall possess the gate of his enemies;' that is, towns and fortresses.* Genesis 22:17 KJV

~ The Gatekeeper's Key: Appendix—Defining Terms ~

KEE'PER:
1. One who keeps; one that holds or has possession of any thing.
2. One who retains in custody; one who has the care of a prison and the custody of prisoners.
3. One who has the care, custody or superintendence of any thing. In Great Britain, the keeper of the great seal, is a lord by his office

KEY:
1. An instrument for shutting or opening a lock, by pushing the bolt one way or the other. Keys are of various forms, and fitted to the wards of the locks to which they belong.
2. In music, the key or key note, is the fundamental note or tone, to which the whole piece is accommodated, and with which it usually begins and always ends.
3. That which serves to explain any thing difficult to be understood.

APPREN'TICE:
1. One who is bound by covenant to serve a mechanic, or other person, for a certain time, with a view to learn his art, mystery, or occupation, in which his master is bound to instruct him. Apprentices are regularly bound by indentures.
2. To bind to, or put under the care of a master, for the purpose of instruction in the knowledge of a trade or business.

~ The Gatekeeper's Key: Appendix—Defining Terms ~

JOUR'NEYMAN:
1. Strictly, a man hired to work by the day
2. One who is hired to work for another in his employment, whether by the month, year or other term . . . in their own occupations.

M'ASTER:
1. A man who rules, governs or directs either men or business . . . who has apprentices and has the government and direction of them. The man who superintends and directs any business, is master or master workman.

    O thou my friend, my genius, come along,
    Thou master of the poet and the song.

2. The director of a school; a teacher; an instructor. In this sense the word is giving place to the more appropriate words teacher, instructor and preceptor;
3. A man eminently or perfectly skilled in any occupation, art or science. We say, a man is master of his business; a great master of music, of the flute or violin; a master of his subject, etc.
4. The word master has numerous applications, in all of which it has the sense of director, chief or superintendent.

BOUND'ARY:
1. A limit; a bound. . . a visible mark designating a limit.

2. Bound is the limit itself or furthest point of extension, and may be an imaginary line; but boundary is the thing which ascertains the limit;

BOUND:
1. A limit; the line which comprehends the whole of any given object or space.
2. A limit by which any excursion is restrained

M'ARGIN:
1. A border; edge; brink; verge;

BORD'ER:
1. The outer edge of any thing; the extreme part or surrounding line; in short, the outer part or edge of things too numerous to be specified.
2. To confine; to touch at the edge,

LIM'IT:
1. Bound; border; utmost extent . . . The thing which bounds; restraint. *They tempted God and limited the Holy One of Israel.* Psalms 78:41 KJV

LAND'MARK:
1. A mark to designate the boundary of land;
2. In navigation, any elevated object on land that serves as a guide to seamen.

FENCE:
1. A wall, hedge, ditch, bank, or line of posts and rails, or of boards or pickets, intended to confine

2. A guard; any thing to restrain entrance; that which defends from attack, approach or injury;
3. To enclose with a hedge, wall, or any thing that prevents the escape or entrance . . . *He hath fenced my way that I cannot pass.* Job 19:8 KJV
4. To guard; to fortify.

WALL:
1. A work or structure of stone, brick or other materials, raised to some height, and intended for a defense or security.
2. A defense; means of security or protection.

THRESH'HOLD:
1. The doorsill . . . Entrance; the place or point of entering or beginning.

Word Study Tips

The *Noah Webster's 1828 Dictionary* won't have contemporary or trendy words as added to the lexicon over the past 175 years. But defining biblical and historical terms, and moral vocabulary, with depth and precision, makes it a necessary and invaluable aid to personal and academic study. The Principle Approach method of word study involves the practice of applying the 4R's: Research, Reasoning, Relating, and Recording.

Within each definition presented here, you'll find "key words." Research the key words within the main word's definition to press deeper into the meaning and usage of the word. This broadens your grasp of it for better Reasoning in how it might Relate to you, the subject being studied, and

~ *The Gatekeeper's Key: Appendix—Defining Terms* ~

God's purposes within its meaning. Record in writing what you learn in a way that is useful to you. A graph is a simple way to work out each of these 4R's at a glance. Here's a sample using the word, FARM, from the *Literature Study Guide* to my book, *Mother Chicken's Eggs: Choosing to Grow into Greater Things*. Do you know what a farm is? Bet you didn't know it could mean as much as it does here:

Fable Springs Study Guide ~ Mother Chicken's Eggs: Choosing to Grow into Greater Things

Word Study Chart Chapter 1 Title Enriching Incubation

Focus Word Defined	Key Words Defined	Restated & Applied to Story
Farm: noun — a portion or tract of land ... cultivated by one man and usually owned by him ... most cultivators are proprietors of the land, and called farmers.	**Farmer: noun** — One who cultivates a farm, a husbandman, whether a tenant or the proprietor.	A FARM is a place where life is CULTIVATED.
Farm: verb — To cultivate land.	**Proprietor: noun** — An owner, the person who has the equal right or exclusive title to any thing whether in possession or not ... By the gift of God man is constituted the proprietor of the earth.	The purpose of living on a farm is to be cultivated to grow into greater things.
Cultivate: verb — 1. To labor on, manage 2. To improve by labor or study, to advance the growth of, to refine by correction of faults, and enlargement of powers or good qualities 3. To cherish, to foster, to promote and increase, 4. To meliorate, to make better, to correct, to civilize, to raise or produce	**Cultivate: verb** — WOW! What a great word! See below for further study! Look at all the great Key Words found in Cultivate as derived from the word Farm: labor, manage, improve, study, advance, growth, refine, enlargement, cherish, foster, promote, increase, make better, correct, civilize, raise, produce **MELIORATE: verb** — To grow better.	Farmer MacDonald's job, as proprietor and owner of his farm, is to see to it that all life on the farm improves, increases, is made better, and is raised up to produce. He will cultivate his farm through his management, labor, and the enlargement of all things good. He cherishes and fosters all the life in his care through the correction and civilizing of faults for the purpose of growing into greater things.

Copyright 2015 Pageant Wagon Publishing

Take hold of My instructions;
don't let them go.
Guard them, for they are the key to life.

Proverbs 4:13 NLT

Notes

Scripture quotations marked NLT are taken from Holy Bible, New Living Translation copyright© 1996, 2004, 2007, 2013 by Tyndale House Foundation. Used by permission of Tyndale House Publishers Inc., Carol Stream, Illinois 60188. All rights reserved.

Scripture quotations marked MSG are taken from The Message, Copyright © 1993, 1994, 1995, 1996, 2000, 2001, 2002 by Eugene H. Peterson

Scripture quotations marked NKJV are taken from the Holy Bible, New King James Version®. Copyright © 1982 by Thomas Nelson. Used by permission. All rights reserved.

Scripture quotations marked KJV are taken from the Holy Bible, King James Version, Public Domain

The American Dictionary of the English Language 1828, by Noah Webster, online version, www.webstersdictionary1828.com

Mansfield Park, by Jane Austen, Penguin Classics

The Door in the Wall, by Marguerite de Angeli, Published by Bantam Doubleday Dell Books for Young Readers a Division of Bantam Doubleday Dell Publishing Group, Inc. New York, New York 10036, Copyright © 1949, 1977

Hinds' Feet in High Places, by Hannah Hurnard, American edition Copyright © 1975, Tyndale House Publishers

The Lion, the Witch, and the Wardrobe, C. S. Lewis, Book Club Edition, Copyright 1950, By the MacMillian Company

The Pilgrim's Progress in Modern English, by John Bunyan, Revised and Updated by L. Edward Hazelbaker, Copyright © 1998 by L. Edward Hazelbaker

Opportunity, by Edward Sill, Public Domain

Good King Wenceslas, by John Mason Neale, Public Domain

To learn more about Principle Approach Education® and the *Foundation for American Christian Education,* visit www.FACE.net.

To learn more about the many Gatekeepers I've met along the way in my writing, speaking, and publishing journey, and the Keys of Opportunity to be found at writing conferences, visit the *Greater Philadelphia Christian Writers Conference* at http://philadelphia.writehisanswer.com/

To hear the audio dramatization version of Chapter 2, *The Gatekeeper's Key,* listen online: http://www.thewritersreverie.com/2016/01/podcast-episode-5-the-gatekeepers-key.html

To explore more about the themes in this book, you may enjoy the high concept picture books, study guides, and audio dramatization CDs in Fable Springs Parables from Pageant Wagon Publishing available online in the Bookshop at www.pageantwagonpublishing.com:

Mother Chicken's Eggs: Choosing to Grow into Greater Things
Theme: The power of free will and how choices have consequences.

Bugaboo-Bee's Bop: Patience for the Prize
Theme: Developing patience while maturing through the ordered steps of life and living—making bitter seasons sweet.

Chapter 7, One Way Through: Jesus—The Ultimate Gatekeeper was inspired in part by Dr. Verdra Jackson and Pastor Sal Roggio.

About the Author

Kathryn "Miss Kathy" Ross, writer, speaker, and dramatist, ignites a love of literature and learning as a family through story and drama. Inspired by the stillness of birdsong, silent reflection, antiques, and teatime, she filters her love of history, classic literature, and the arts through God's Word, to inform her words. Old world elegance and a vintage hat distinguishes her captivating stage presence in speaking to women's groups and family audiences.

> *"My prayer is that through the written and spoken word, I may lead you into the presence of the Lord, then step out of the way and allow the teaching ministry of the Holy Spirit to do His divine work of drawing you deeper into the intimacy of His truth and love in Christ Jesus."*

Trained in Principle Approach® Education through the Foundation for American Christian Education, Miss Kathy previously taught in Christian and homeschool settings, and provides enrichment programs in public schools. She specializes in writing and publishing curriculum tools for homeschoolers and church discipleship, promoting a Family Literacy Lifestyle—reading together, learning together, loving together—all ages, all at the same time.

Miss Kathy is the author/owner of Pageant Wagon Publishing. She designs story-worlds spanning the likes of an idyllic English country village to a Wild West gold rush town. In addition to her diverse inspirational speaking and teaching topics.

Blogs and podcasts original works plus literacy related posts at
TheWritersReverie.com
Publishing website plus the Family Literacy Lifestyle Blog at
PageantWagonPublishing.com
Contact Miss Kathy at **info@pageantwagonpublishing.com** to learn more about her speaking programs and fees.

Inspiration from Pageant Wagon Publishing

Inspirational Christian Living
for Journaling, Discussion Groups, and Bible Study

Coming in 2018

On the west coast of Italy, the cameo masters have turned abandoned shells pulled from the depths of the sea into cherished works of art, worn as ornamental jewelry and prized as keepsake family heirlooms for centuries. Follow Cassie's journey as she submits to the master's chisel and learns the cost of being set apart for greater glory.

By Kathryn Ross

Available from Amazon or order direct from
www.pageantwagonpublishing.com

Homeschool and Literacy Enrichment from Pageant Wagon Publishing

Fable Springs Parables
High-concept Picture Books and Study Guides

Literacy Journals and Theatrical Scripts
for Home, Schools, and Churches

Pageant Wagon Publishing provides biblically based storybooks, study guides, drama scripts, homeschool enrichment, and devotional works to promote a Family Literacy Lifestyle through Christian discipleship for home, church, and classroom.

Visit us online to order books and learn more:
www.pageantwagonpublishing.com
Blogging at www.thewritersreverie.com

The Speaking Ministry of Kathryn Ross

Speaking Events for women and families feature displays, PowerPoint visuals, interactive elements, and more!

The Gatekeeper's Key
Cross the threshold to fulfilling God's call on your life.

Fragrant Fields
Devotions through performance poetry and prose.

The Cameo Christian
Becoming a work of art, raised up and set apart to shine.

Fable Springs Parables
Family ministry through the power of story.

Hats Off to the Ladies Teatime
Rediscovering femininity through millinery history.

Dramatized Classic Literature
Meet Jane Austen, Charles Dickens, C. S. Lewis, and more!

Listen online to Miss Kathy's dramatized audio stories and essays at *The Writer's Reverie*
www.thewritersreverie.com
Click on **PODCASTS**

Contact Miss Kathy for performance fees and booking info:
info@pageantwagonpublishing.com

www.ingramcontent.com/pod-product-compliance
Lightning Source LLC
LaVergne TN
LVHW041546070426
835507LV00011B/952